Forgotten Heroines of the North East

by Mike Gibb

Acknowledgements

A huge thank you to all at the Doric Board for their generous support of this book.

Thanks to Cynthia Burek, Deputy Director Centre for Science Communication at the University of Chester for copies of papers she has written about Maria Ogilvie Gordon and Penny Hartley of the College Archives Department of Robert Gordon's College.

Thanks also to author Daniel Gray for his assistance with information and photographs of Annie Murray.

As always I am grateful to my long time collaborator, the highly talented graphic artist David Stout for designing the great cover and for helping with the layout of the book.

Anyone interested on finding out more about some of the women in this book should check out the following:

Mary Garden by Michael T.R.B. Turnbull (Scolar Press)

Homage to Caledonia by Daniel Gray (Luath Press)

Mary Slessor by Elizabeth Robertson (NMS Publishing)

The Collected Works of Lorna Moon edited by Glenda Norquay (Black & White Books)

For further information on any of writer Mike Gibb other books (full list on page 4) email mikegibb32@outlook.com

To HELENA.

All Best Wishes.

This book is dedicated to my own never forgotten heroines

Beth, Kirsty and Rebecca

By the same writer

Musical Plays

A Land Fit For Heroes

Mother of All the Peoples

Five Pound & Twa Bairns

Sunday Mornings on Dundee Law

Clarinda

Red Harlaw

Aberdeen's Forgotten Diva

Outlander the Musical

As Long As But A Hundred Of Us

Plays

Children of the Sea

Lest We Forget

Doorways in Drumorty

Giacomo & Glover

Books

It's A Dawgs Life

Waiting For the Master

Ask Anna

How To Train Your Owner

Anna's Adventures In Wonderland

When Angus Met Donny

Sammy the Tammy (The Mystery of the Missing Mascot)

The Name's Sammy, Sammy the Tammy

Drumorty Revisited

Just Another Seterday in Dundee

Introduction

When I read that Aberdeen were to honour the city's famous sons and daughters in a Hall of Heroes in the recently refurbished Provost Skene House I was delighted; delighted until the list of "heroes" was published. Where were Mary Slessor and Mary Garden, both of whom were born less than a mile from the historic building?

The omission of Mary Slessor was particularly disappointing. In 2018 the general public were asked to vote for the women they wanted included in the new Hall of Heroes in the National Wallace Monument in Stirling and top of the list was Mary, revered by the populace of Scotland, ignored by her native city.

That situation set me thinking of other women from this corner of Scotland who were now "forgotten", shunned in favour of this year's, or at least this century's, model.

And so I decided to try to rectify the situation to a limited degree by producing this little book that shines a 21st century light on five women from a much earlier era who undoubtedly deserve to be remembered. Women from very different backgrounds who excelled in totally diverse ways but who all had one thing in common.

They were all willing to show great determination and courage by leaving their native North East to venture afar with a mission to infiltrate and excel in a world that was largely male dominated. All of them succeeded remarkably which makes it all the more unfortunate that they are remembered by so few in an era where opportunities for women are so different from their 19th Century predecessors.

These are very much potted, and hopefully entertaining, bios of these colourful characters that will encourage the readers to seek out the many fine books covering in far greater depth the lives of these forgotten heroines.

Mary Garden
(1874-1967)

From Charlotte Street to Times Square

The mighty steam train stopped at the buffers and disgorged its passengers onto Platform 1 of Aberdeen's Joint Station. They were a motley collection. Smartly dressed suited gentleman returning from business trips to London, garishly dressed families coming from a day out to the Beach at Stonehaven and a miscellany of others.

Amidst the bustling multitude was an elegant, beautifully dressed elderly lady completing the final leg of an epic journey that had begun with the Queen Mary sailing out of the harbour of New York City. She had just finished an extensive lecture tour around America where she had been mobbed by admirers and devotees at every venue. And yet as she walked sedately across the Station concourse she was ignored by both her fellow passengers and those waiting to greet them. Only one person paid the lady any attention; Agnes, her sister.

The lady in question, returning to her native city, was Mary Garden, the finest and most famous opera singer the U.K. has ever produced.

There is a scene in the movie *Quartet* where three of the residents (played by Billy Connolly, Tom Courtney and Pauline Collins) of Beecham House, a home for retired performers, are eagerly awaiting the arrival of a new resident, aware that it is a person of great distinction. In speculating just who it could be, one of them suggest jokingly "perhaps it is Mary Garden". That is just an example of how huge an opera star she was.

Yet her native city has paid her scant regard. There is small yellow plaque on the home in Dee Street where she lived part of her early life and a small stone monument, often poorly tended and consequently partially obscured by growing shrubs, and a simple park bench on Craigie Loanings, near to Belgrave Terrace, her last home in the city. Sadly the commemorative plaque and photograph that once could be seen at the coffee bar in the Music Hall, giving rise to the room being informally referred to as the "Mary Garden Room", were thrown away during the recent refurbishment of the building and despite strenuous efforts by aficionados were never replaced.

Mary was born on 20 February 1874 although she subsequently declared that her birth year was 1877, possibly choosing this later date in light of the fact that her Mother and Father were married in January 1874. This was only one of many inaccuracies that appeared in Mary's 1951 autobiography, *Mary Garden's Story* where she suggested that she had spent much of her childhood at her grandfather's country mansion and 1000 acre estate called Pitmurchie House, Torphins. Sadly the Garden family were never that well to do, although her sister Amy did marry into money and inherited that particular property. In fact Mary spent her early childhood in a tenement flat in Charlotte Street before moving with her parents and three sisters to Dee Street.

Plaque on the house in Dee Street, Aberdeen

In 1880, the six year old Mary, along with her siblings and mother paid a fond farewell to Robert Garden who was experiencing difficulty in providing for his expanded family and set off for

America looking for work with the intention of sending for his wife and children once he was settled and financially sound. It was, however, three long years before he was able to afford to bring Mary and the others to America. The Gardens initially stayed in Brooklyn before moving to Massachusetts but in 1889 returned to Aberdeen for a year, Mary and her sisters enrolling at the City's St. Margaret's School for Girls.

When the time came to return to America they headed for the vibrant city of Chicago which Mary loved and it was here that she developed the bug for both acting and singing. It soon became clear that she possessed real talent and a local singing teacher was highly impressed by her pupil, so much so that after the Garden family moved again, firstly to Hartford, Connecticut and subsequently to Philadelphia, where Robert Garden established a successful bicycle sale and repair business, Mary happily returned to Chicago to continue her musical training.

She made such remarkable strides in her studies that a sponsor, a Mrs Florence Mayer, who was married to a wealthy Chicago businessman, was so highly impressed by the young protégé that she provided funding for Mary and Mrs Duff, her tutor, to go to Paris to study and in 1896, aged 22, Mary arrived in the French capital.

Armed with a generous grant from her benefactors back in the States, Mary began taking lessons from a leading operatic teacher. And then another one. And another. Whatever the reasons the somewhat precocious Mary and her tutors just didn't see eye to eye and in the early months of her time in Paris the only thing that Mary seemed to excel at was spending her sponsor's money on a fairly gregarious and relatively lavish lifestyle. Sadly word of this got back to the Mayer family in Chicago who curtly advised her in a letter there would be no more money coming to support her as Mary's "conduct was not as we had supposed".

In truth there was probably another reason for the decision. Ed Mayer, the young son of Mary's benefactors, had gone to Paris and Mary and him became such good friends that talk of an engagement was in the air. This was not something that would have thrilled the Mayers who had no wish to see their darling son married off to a "theatrical" and so the plug was pulled on Mary's only source of income.

By this time Mary had found a tutor she respected and had no wish to leave Paris and so she succeeded in sweet talking both her landlady and her singing teacher into extending her credit. Sadly all too soon their patience ran out and she found herself literally locked out of her apartment with her meagre few sticks of furniture and other possessions retained to help offset her debt, and with no access to her tutor. She located a room elsewhere until, once again, she was evicted for non payment of rent and was in truly desperate straits when fate decided to intervene.

She was walking in Paris, trying to conjure up a solution to her problems when she passed a lady dressed in mourning garb. Although she didn't recognise the person because of her attire, she did know her dogs. It was Sibyl Sanderson, an American soprano to whom Mary had been introduced the previous year and Mary stopped and spoke to her.

Despite her own less than happy situation – Sibyl was in mourning for her husband who had recently died and was in poor health herself – she instantly took Mary under her wing. Mary had described Sibyl after that initial meeting as "simply charming, beautiful, fascinating and clever". Now she could clearly add kind and compassionate, not epithets that would necessarily apply to many of her contemporaries. Sibyl ushered Mary to her carriage and took her to her apartment.

Without Sibyl Sanderson's benevolence and caring, Mary would probably have ended up back in the States and the world of opera might have been deprived of one of its greatest talents for Sibyl not only gave Mary somewhere to stay but also cleared all her debts and recovered her paltry possessions. Just as importantly she introduced Mary to Albert Carre, the manager of the Opera-Comique in Paris.

Based on Sibyl's recommendation Carre agreed to audition Mary Garden but he was less than impressed with her French pronunciation. However, he must have spotted something special in the young girl as he offered her a small part in a production of *Carmen* as well as free access to the theatre. And Mary certainly took full advantage of that offer, attending the building more or less every day especially during the time that they were rehearsing a new opera titled *Louise,* written by Gustave Charpentier. Spotting Mary's obvious love of the piece Monsieur Carre provided her with a copy of the libretto suggesting that she study it. Mary didn't do just that; she devoured it and before long she knew the title role by heart.

Mary in the role of Louise

The opera opened and proved to be a great critical and commercial success. But then the diva playing the part of Louise fell ill. Not a major problem it seemed as there was an understudy standing by to take over the role; well not a major problem until the understudy came down with a severe cold and expressed reservations about whether her voice would hold up through all three acts. One can only imagine the scene in the theatre after they received that news until someone piped up:

Mary Garden can sing it sir!

The chorus girl?

Yes indeed, straight out of *The Phantom of the Opera.*

In actual fact Mary's debut wasn't quite that spectacular as Monsieur Carre, aware that Mary had learned the part, had involved her in a number of rehearsals prior to that fateful day. But it certainly had its fair share of drama arising from a phone call made by the theatre management to Sibyl's home where Mary was still staying. Both Mary and Sibyl were in very low spirits following the tragic death of one of the dogs when the phone rang and was answered by the hostess.

Yes she is here. No she certainly can't.

Realising that they were talking about her and establishing that the caller was Monsieur Carre who was enquiring that, if required, could she sing *Louise* that night, Mary flew across the room and grabbed the phone.

Monsieur Carre, this is Mary and I certainly CAN sing Louise tonight.

And so, dressed in a costume beneath her cloak and accompanied by Sibyl and Sibil's sisters, Mary made her way to the theatre that evening. Now in her infamous autobiography Mary, in best superstitious mode, states that the date was April 13th (1890) and that she was seated in the stalls in seat 113, In actual fact it was 10th April and she was in Box 17. Her book is often a stranger to the truth but is seldom less than entertaining.

Mary and her friends sat in their box through the first two acts of the opera as the understudy valiantly coped with the demands of the eponymous role; one can only speculate that the rather ambitious Mary had revelled in every slightly croaky note. Eventually at the end of act two, the diva declared "I can't go on", probably with the back of her hand pressed to her forehead in best dramatic fashion, and the curtain to the side of the box occupied by Miss Garden parted and she was summoned back stage.

An announcement was made to the clearly disappointed audience and before Mary had time to catch her breath, she found herself centre stage facing a mass of patrons, mainly in their best evening wear, waiting expectantly to see what this girl could do. She began slightly shakily, which is hardly surprisingly in the circumstances, but soon found her feet which was just as well as she was suddenly faced with the opera's big aria.

Depuis le jour (*Since the day*) is an aria that has been sung by pretty well all the top female opera stars over the years including the likes of Maria Callas and, more recently, Renee Fleming so it was a great deal to ask of a slip of a girl making her major stage debut. But, of course, Mary Garden was no ordinary slip of a girl. She performed it with such grace and beauty that she brought the house down or as she herself put it more elegantly, 'the sound of the audience applause was like rain on a tin roof'.

She sailed through the remainder of the act and took her bows to shouts of bravo and of 'Marygardenne' while programmes and handkerchiefs were waved and some of the ecstatic audience even threw themselves onto the stage. Andre Messager, the orchestra conductor, gestured to the musicians to stand and held his baton in the air, the greatest compliment a conductor can pay an artist.

Mary went home to her little bedroom and declared that "my eyes wouldn't shut. I would put my fingers over them and close them oh so tight and – pouf – they would fly open". A star was born and if she was on cloud nine that night, she must have been even more delighted the next morning when she picked up the newspapers. They were universally complimentary with *Le Figaro* (France's most prominent daily) asserting that she "had a delightful voice and pleasing appearance which quickly won over the audience".

Although Mary would go on to star in a host of leading roles in her lengthy and illustrious career, the role of *Louise* was the one she performed most, 175 times in total in fact. And not surprisingly the aria *Dupois le Jour* always remained special to her and she recorded it several times, released by RCA Victrola as a cylinder and subsequently as a 78 rpm disc and now to be found as the opening track on *The Complete RCA Recordings* CD.

Carre obviously recognised talent and wasted no time in getting Mary under contract, offering her a decent monthly wage which she was delighted to accept, not surprising in light of the fact that months earlier she was homeless and penniless. But a little while later Monsieur Carre, who was recently divorced, had another type of contract in mind and proposed to Mary. When she turned him down, explaining that there was another man in her life (Messager, the conductor, with whom it appears she was having an affair) Carre ripped up her contract in a fit of pique.

Fortunately for Mary she had received an offer from the prestigious La Scala in Milan to sing *Louise* and when Carre learned of this he very quickly proffered a new contract which Mary signed. Clearly when it came right down to it Mary's attraction as the new darling of French opera outweighed her attractions as a wife.

The Opera-Comique closed in the summer which gave Mary the opportunity to get away from the city and to head to the spa town of Aix-les-Bains where she premiered a new opera by composer Jules Massenet titled *Thais*. On her return she moved into an apartment of her own in Paris, as although she would always be eternally grateful to Sibyl, she had become increasingly concerned by her behaviour which included alcoholic binges and possibly even drug taking. The new apartment was not the height of luxury, being on the fifth floor of a building, but it gave her privacy and it had a small balcony with pleasing views over her adopted Paris.

Carre, despite the disappointment of being shunned romantically, continued to promote his discovery getting her to audition for Claude Debussy, the man now regarded as arguably France's greatest classical composer, thanks to works like *Clair de Lune* and *La Mer.* Debussy was in the process of writing an opera titled *Pelleas et Melisande,* which proved to be the only full length opera that the great composer ever completed.

Mary in the role of Melisande

After an evening with a number of fellow opera performers during which time Debussy played through the complete score, Mary was invited to attend the Opera Comique and asked, by a rather off handed

Debussy who was despairing of finding the right leading lady, to sing. After Mary had sung the complete first two acts and had begun the third, Debussy stopped playing and left the room without saying a word, leaving a confused and somewhat crestfallen Mary.

Mary was then summoned to Carre's office where she discovered that Debussy was seated. The composer stood and grasped both of Mary's hands before saying "You have come all the way from the cold North to create my music". And so Mary Garden became Melisande, much to the chagrin of librettist Maurice Maeterlinck as he was under great pressure from his mistress to get her cast.

Following the success of that role Mary suddenly found herself in great demand and within months was singing in the likes of Monte Carlo and the Royal Opera House in Covent Garden, the first of several visits to that celebrated venue. Initially she enjoyed the London experience but after appearing there while suffering from a cold, as a consequence of which both the press and the audiences were less than impressed by her performance, her mood changed. "I loathe London. The atmosphere of the place is always frightfully depressing. I don't love the English."

But away from London her career was going from strength to strength and everything in the garden seemed rosy until a tragedy occurred which deeply affected her. Her great friend and benefactor Sibyl Sanderson died suddenly and Mary, in her grief, reflected on the fact that Sibyl had rescued her when she was at her lowest ebb personally and professionally. Mind you that didn't stop her going to Sibyl's apartment on the day after the funeral and helping herself to many of the lady's operatic costumes and stage jewellery.

The following year Mary was back in London, this time to appear with a cast of stars of the opera world at a gala evening being staged at Windsor Castle by King Edward VII for the visiting King George of Greece. Mary sang what was fast becoming her signature tune *Dupois le Jour* as well as a song from *Tosca,* sharing the stage with many others including the legendary Nellie Melba who, at the end of the evening, told the assembled company "What a poor concert this would have been if I had not been singing". Most of the other artists were less than impressed by Melba's outburst but Mary laughed it off and, having travelled back to London together, they quickly became firm friends. Mind you, it is not hard to understand why Mary was in a particularly magnanimous humour that evening; King George of Greece, who had long been an admirer of Mary's work and a regular attendee at her performances at Aix-les-Bains, presented her with a pearl necklace, subsequent valued at $1.5 million.

Mary's new found wealth meant that she could afford to employee a maid and one she used as a first line of defence to avoid unwelcome visitors. One day a gentleman of advancing years climbed the five flights of stairs to reach Mary's apartment and had to sit on the top step for a few minutes to regain his breath. When he knocked on the door it was opened by the maid whom informed him that "Mademoiselle Garden is resting and is too tired to see anyone". He presented his card and left.

Oscar Hammerstein

It was only later that Mary realised that the visitor had been a certain Oscar Hammerstein, New York's most famous impresario.

Hammerstein (the father of the gentleman of the same name who enjoyed great success as a writer of musicals with composer Richard Rodgers) was a German immigrant who made his fortune as cigar maker before opening a series of theatres in New York.

The first of these was the Harlem Opera House on 125th Street followed by the Columbus Theatre, the Manhattan Opera House and the Olympia Theatre, the last named being built on Longacre Square, now better known as Times Square. Another three theatres followed before, in 1906, he opened a second Manhattan Opera House and it was this event that brought him to Paris.

Determined to compete with the prominent Metropolitan Opera House, he came over from America to acquire the rights to the operas *Louise* and *Pelleas et Melisande,* and having done so, to persuade the famous diva to perform these in New York. Despite the somewhat inauspicious start, Hammerstein and Garden did meet up and before long Mary was packing her trunks, all sixteen of them, no doubt partially filled with her departed friend's costumes, and heading back to the U.S.A. On her arrival she was met by her father, now a successful automobile dealer, and large posse of press reporters.

Manhattan Opera House

Mary always had a unique relationship with the press who loved the fact that she could nearly always be relied on to come up with some colourful and on occasions slightly risqué comment. On her first press conference on her return to American soil she was asked what parts she would like to play and she launched into a spiel about her admiration for Wagner and how she would love to sing *Tristan and Isolde*. "But you can't sing Isolde until you have had many affairs?" one reporter suggested. "I fancy I can manage that" was Mary's response. In fact she never performed this role or any other by Wagner.

This was the beginning of a long and successful career in America although her work was loved by many, ridiculed by some. What seems to be clear is that Mary brought great dramatic strength to the roles which she not so much played as inhabited but perhaps didn't quite have the quality of voice of the very best divas. Some critics, and most audience members, revelled in the theatricality she brought to the stage but *The New York Globe*, somewhat unkindly, suggested that "her singing was a hindrance rather than an aid".

During the first quarter of the 20th century Mary was sailing back and forth from the U.S.A. to Europe and vice versa on an annual basis. During one of her European visits she travelled to Germany to meet composer Richard Strauss, whose work she loved, and discussed the possibility of her playing the role of *Salome* in a new opera of the same name that Strauss was writing. Because of the subject matter and with its notorious dance of the seven veils, Mary knew that it would be hugely controversial but that simply made her even more determined to secure the part. The composer was clearly impressed by the singer and she was given the chance to make the role her own on the stage of the Manhattan Opera House and returned to New York in early 1909 to do just that.

She sailed into a sea of controversy, not about Salome but totally of her own making. Discovering that Hammerstein was intending to give the lead part of the opera *Thais,* a role she regarded as hers, to the Italian Lina Cavalieri, she voiced her displeasure to the impresario in no uncertain terms with the wonderful line "I will not allow an Italian to sing my French roles", seemingly ignoring the fact she herself was in fact Scottish!.

She took the dispute a stage further by failing to turn up for *Salome* rehearsal, leaving an orchestra of 115 players twiddling their violin bows. Hammerstein soon got the message and poor Ms. Cavalieri was suddenly struck down with some undefined illness that left her unable to sing. Garden 1 Hammerstein 0.

**Mary in the controversial role of Salome
with the head of John the Baptist**

In late January Mary took to the stage as *Salome* with a performance that totally slayed the citizens of New York who sat riveted by her acting and singing and even dancing; unlike most of the divas who later presented the role, Mary insisted on performing the infamous dance herself rather than using a double. When the curtain fell the audience sat in stunned silence for all of 30 seconds before voicing their acclaim. After the success in New York it was on to Philadelphia and straight into a torrent of protests from Churches of all denominations. On the other hand a local nudist group, the Sunshiners, were delighted declaring "We look upon it as the greatest force for true morality that has ever come to Philadelphia" seemingly unaware that the costume that Mary wore was rather more modest than they assumed and expected.

Over the course of her lengthy career Mary would don the cloak, or rather the seven veils, of *Salome* a total of sixty one times with wildly differing reactions. In Paris they were well acquainted with the opera and when Mary returned to perform it, there were in fact no less than three different productions running cheek by jowl with three divas interpreting the part in different ways. Clearly the somewhat more broadminded French had a liking for the story unlike the citizens, or at least the Police Chief, of Chicago who described her performance as "disgusting ...Garden wallowed around like a cat in a bed of catnip". Someone obviously agreed with his views, sending Mary a "gift" in the form of a bag of catnip. The end result was that the opera closed early and was banned by Baltimore.

After much discussion Milwaukee allowed it to proceed and all the publicity did nothing to harm ticket sales. However, many theatre goers, hoping for an evening of titillation, left disappointed, considering it tame while the local newspaper described it as "grand opera gone quite mad".

In 1911 she received a request to undertake a major concert tour of cities along the Eastern Seaboard of America together with a few Western dates. She initially turned down the offer because she was "writing my autobiography" (the book was eventually published almost forty years later) but was persuaded by the offer of a private Pullman railway car together with three porters, a chef brought in from Paris, two maids, a secretary, a literary assistant to whom she could dictate and even a security guard to look after her jewellery. The tour was generally successful and provided her with the opportunity of performing in Carnegie Hall, the celebrated venue built by the Scottish industrialist Andrew Carnegie, a man who Mary met and befriended on one of her many trips across the Atlantic.

Throughout her life many column inches were devoted to Mary's love life and in particular her "impending marriage", with the press linking her with a wide variety of men from various walks of life, even a member of the royalty, Prince Mavrocordato, a wealthy Russian living in Paris. He was clearly bewitched by Mary, occupying a box in any Paris theatre where she was performing and leaving the theatre if it transpired that Mary wasn't appearing that evening.

Despite the fact that romance was clearly in the air, Mary never became Princess Mavrocordato or in fact Mistress anything, living out her life as a single woman, albeit one with an abundance of male friends and admirers. Possibly the nearest she came to giving up her maiden name was with a fellow opera star, known as Vanni-Marcoux with rumours starting when they were frequently to be seen lunching at the fashionable Copley Plaza Hotel and catching fire when they appeared together on stage in *Tosca,* their steamy on stage scenes engendering complaints from the Mayor of Boston and members of the public.

During that same era Mary set off on a major U.S. tour with the Chicago Grand Opera Company, arriving in Los Angeles with 42 trunks of clothes and costumes. She took over nine rooms in a local hotel to accommodate her, her mother and her maids but was a little put out when she discovered that her co-star, Luisa Terazzani had outdone her by booking eleven rooms. The era just before the outbreak of the Great War was by far the most successful in Mary's many years on stage, with success after success. But it wasn't all sunshine and roses.

Over the years she had built up a huge following of devotees, one of whom was a nineteen year old girl called Helen Newby, the daughter of industrialist from Pennsylvania. The young girl was totally obsessed with Mary and on one occasion travelled to Philadelphia to see her idol. Helen was able to watch Mary on stage two nights in succession but this was clearly not enough to quench her sense of adoration and she tried to get back stage but without success. Undaunted she went to the Ritz Carlton Hotel after the second show and asked for an interview. Mary was at the time looking after her mother who was ill and the girl was turned away in tears.

The following morning her body was discovered in the garden of her home. She had shot herself in the head with a revolver and hidden inside her dress was a photo of Mary Garden. When the story was broken to Mary by a local newspaper she was shocked and upset and no doubt felt a sense of guilt despite the fact that she had never met the girl and was regularly besieged at the stage door night after night by her adoring public.

Mary at the height of her fame

In 1914 the world changed dramatically for many people with the outbreak of war and no more so than for Mary Garden. She was in the U.S. when war was declared but somewhat bravely decided to return to Paris and to take fairly dramatic action to help her beloved France, dressing up as a young boy and trying to enlist in the army. The General commanding the regiment she tried to join was somewhat suspicious, believing that the "boy" could be a German spy, and a full examination was ordered which naturally revealed that the young lad was none other than Mary Garden. She later confirmed that this strange story, first reported in the New York Review, was true; "I owe France more than I ever can repay, even by giving my life, and I am sure that I could fight as well as any man if only they would let me."

That ploy having failed Mary decided to do her bit for the war effort by working as a nurse for the Red Cross, turning her car into an ambulance to bring back injured servicemen from the front, and also helped to run a refuge for women and children housed in an old chateau, while also appearing at concerts to raise money for the war effort and in particular for the Serbian Red Cross.

As the four long years of war were at last drawing to a close Mary suddenly found herself being pursued by the movie mogul Sam Goldwyn who thought he had spotted a new star of the silver screen. Goldwyn was born in Warsaw and left there without a zloty to his name, travelling around Europe and working at a variety of jobs before heading for the States and establishing a film studio with a group of men that included Cecil B. DeMille. Incidentally when he first left his native Poland he changed his given name of Gelbfisz to Samuel Goldfish but changed it again, somewhat wisely, to Goldwyn. After many successes he became part of the movie picture conglomerate Metro-Goldwyn-Mayer or MGM as it better known today.

Mary was signed up by Goldwyn Pictures to make four movies (although for reasons which will become apparent, only two were made) and was offered a fee of $150,000. Not surprisingly Mary jumped at the chance and sailed once again to America where she began filming in New York. The first movie was titled *Thais* and was an adaption of one of her greatest operatic successes but unfortunately what worked on stage with sound didn't work on film with not a word or note heard.

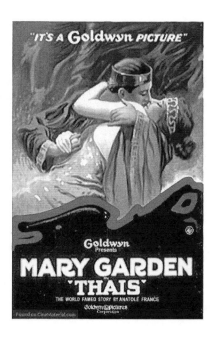

The movie was savaged with one critic describing it as "so tawdry, so crude, so vulgar. Mary Garden brings to the screen the tedious and dismal technique of operatic acting, which is not acting at all but slow motions made while waiting for the music to catch up the with the drama". Somewhat stoically Mary accepted the criticism on the chin suggesting that the film had been ruined by savage cutting and that her next movie would be better. It wasn't.

The Splendid Sinner was based on elements of Mary's own life intertwined with that of Edith Cavell, the British nurse who helped allied soldiers escape from the Germans and who was subsequently executed by firing squad. Despite the dramatic and interesting storyline the film flopped and its failure seems to sit pretty firmly on the shoulders of Mary Garden if the critical response it received is to be believed "She who is gracious, lovely and full of personality on the stage, is minus every one of those qualities on the screen".

One small plus from her unfortunate dalliance with the film industry was the fact that it brought her name to the citizens of her native Aberdeen, who until then seemed unimpressed by her opera success, with the movies being shown at the New Electric Theatre on Union Street, a building which subsequently became the Capitol. Fit the folk o' Aiberdein thoucht o' the quine up on the big screen is nae kent. Perhaps, fortunately.

A clear demonstration of how big a star Mary was at the height of her fame is provided in the form of *Time* magazine. In 1930 the magazine, which boasted the largest circulation of any weekly news magazine anywhere in the world, decided to produce an issue primarily dedicated to the world of opera. And, yes, they chose our Mary as their cover girl.

Following her sojourn into the not so wonderful world of movies, Mary returned to the place that she felt most at home. France. She already had an apartment in Monte Carlo and she bought a villa on the Cote de Azur in the picturesque Mediterranean town of Beaulieu-sur-Mer, which under the fictional name of Beaumont-sur-Mer was the setting for the Michael Caine and Steve Martin movie, *Dirty Rotten Scoundrels*. One summer there she became friendly with Cole Porter and his wife and was introduced to the future mayor of Peille, a small village perched on the mountains between Monaco and Menton.

He explained to Mary how the people of Peille wanted to erect a memorial to the villagers who had been killed in the Great War. Mary instantly donated 9500 francs but with a stipulation; it must be a pacifist monument with the words "tu ne tueras"(thou shalt not kill) inscribed on it. She returned the following summer to see how the construction work was proceeding on what subsequently was called La Palace Mary Garden, with the road leading to it named Avenue Mary Garden. During that visit she was officially declared godmother of the village and her generosity not only extended to paying for the memorial but also helped improve village services such as lighting and drainage.

The war memorial in Peille

In April 1925 she was back in Peille again, this time accompanied by her long term friend and former personal assistant William Chauncey and together they were godparents to a child that had just been born in the village. Sadly that was the last time that the two of them would be there as months later Bill Chauncey injured his foot while swimming and died from the infection that set in. Mary was devastated and requested that he be buried beneath the monument in Peille. Her request was refused as although Chauncey had been a General, he had not died in combat; the villagers did, however, honour him by naming a street General Chauncey Avenue. Clearly Mary bore no grudge about her initial request being refused as she gave the village a further 35,000 francs, a substantial sum in the 1920's.

Mary Garden perfume and cosmetic products

Mary also entered into a contract with the French company Parfumeries Rigaud to produce a Mary Garden perfume although this venture didn't end well with Mary taking them to court when, without her approval, Rigaud began to retail a whole range of cosmetic items with Mary's name and photograph.

Mary had a long association with the Chicago Grand Opera Company and when the director Cleofonte Campanini died suddenly, Mary was persuaded to return to the city to take over that post. Unfortunately her abilities on stage far exceeded those behind the scenes and in her first year in charge the company lost a staggering $1,000,000. All too soon Mary was back where she truly belonged; treading the boards in a wide variety of roles, albeit with a much lighter schedule dictated by her advancing years.

Her final US operatic performance was in Chicago, playing the part of Anita in Massenet's *La Navarraise*. On the fourth and final night of the run she took her bows, left the theatre without a word of farewell to anyone and never looked back. Over the course of more than thirty years she had made over a thousand appearances in numerous operas by many composers including the doyens of the genre like Puccini, Verdi, Bizet and many more.

In the 1930's Mary largely devoted her time to giving concerts and lectures including a complete course at the Chicago Musical College for budding opera students. She also took an advisory role with MGM, travelling to Hollywood to act as a consultant on musical movies and fortunately didn't pursue too vigorously a thankfully brief career in Vaudeville, a drastic departure for her appearances on the grand opera stage.

Shortly before the Second World War broke out in Europe in 1939, Mary had headed back to France; in later years she reckoned she had made the trans-Atlantic crossing more than fifty times in all weathers and during the period of the war in constant danger of attack. It was her intention to remain there during those turbulent years but when in 1940 Paris fell to the Nazis she realised that it was time to flee and was fortunate in getting a seat on one of the last non military planes to depart France. She was forced to leave behind the bulk of her possessions and later discovered that the Germans had commandeered her five cars as well as occupying her Paris home.

She returned to her native Aberdeen and took up residence at 18 Albert Street where she continued to work on the famous autobiography. She became a very regular visitor to His Majesty's Theatre in Aberdeen meeting with a variety of touring actors and performers including Noel Coward, a fact that is recollected by the playwright in his own autobiography, recounting a meeting with Mary in 1942 when one of his plays was on that stage.

Mary Garden, as dynamic as ever, came to the plays and I saw to it that she was treated as royalty. In my opinion she was one of the greatest operatic actresses in the world...she said gaily that she had given up singing forever and preferred smoking and bridge.

But Mary's involvement with that particular theatre again displayed her generous side with Mary regularly buying up blocks of tickets for His Majesty's and handing them out to servicemen injured or on leave.

When the war ended Mary was on her travels again, accepting an invitation in 1948 to undertake a major lecture tour in America and she must have been moved and overwhelmed by the reception she enjoyed on her return. Newspapers and magazines showered her with accolades, numerous hotel suites were named in her honour and several thousand letters and telegrams welcoming her back greeted her arrival.

On her arrival and in best theatrical tradition Mary didn't disappoint, dressing in a Stewart tartan suit to emphasise her Scottish roots and topping off her outfit with a red hat with a large green feather. In addition to various items of jewellery, including the ever present pearls, she also wore the decorations of the Legion d'Honneur and the Croix de Reconnaisssance (known as the medal of French gratitude), awarded by the French Government in recognition of her war time service to her adopted country.

Mary during the era of the U.S. lecture tours

The tour was relatively successful and certainly created an appetite for more and in the early fifties Mary returned a further three times to America, travelling the length and breadth of the country and addressing adoring fans. When not in America she was at home beavering away on the book she had been working on for decades. At last she finished it, or so she thought, and sent it to a critic in New York who in turn showed it to a publisher. Both were savage in their appraisal, suggesting that there was insufficient coverage of her personal life and in particular her countless love affairs. With the assistance of her sister Amy, she worked on re-writes and in 1950 she sent a version to two of her New York publishers who were still not impressed.

They decided that the only way forward was to employ a ghost writer and Louis Biancolli, an author in his own right with a host of books to his name and a music critic for the New York World-Telegram and Sun came onboard. He spent weeks and weeks in Mary's company, making copious notes and at last *Mary Garden's Story,* as it was somewhat unimaginatively titled, was published in 1951 in America and the following year in the UK.

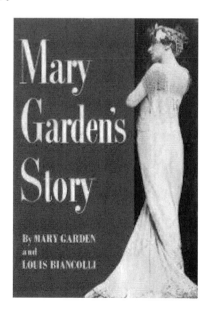

Unfortunately despite the ghost writer's best efforts it was still not well received in certain quarters, with reviewers picking up on the countless inaccuracies. It remains a matter of debate as to whether Mary changed dates and events to make her life even more interesting and glamorous, although that was hardly necessary, or whether the problems arose from the fact that by the time the book was published Mary was in her mid-seventies and was showing the first signs of dementia.

In 1962 Scottish Opera staged a production of *Pelleas et Melisande* to mark the 100th anniversary of the birth of Claude Debussy and invited Mary to the opening night as their guest of honour. Sadly Mary fell shortly before the event breaking both her arms and was unable to attend. While in hospital recovering a number of the other patients asked her to sing for them. At first she declined but eventually, seated on a chair, she sang "Annie Laurie" unaccompanied. When she finished she looked around at the small gathering to see that several people had been reduced to tears.

The fall and the injury marked the beginning of a sharp decline and with the dementia growing steadily worse she was forced to move from her home, a flat on Belgrave Terrace in the Rosemount area of Aberdeen she had moved to in the nineteen fifties, to the House of Daviot Hospital near Oldmeldrum. She had many visitors and mail arrived from all parts of the world. Sadly her mental condition deteriorated so rapidly that she became very difficult and eventually for her own safety had to be strapped to a bed. It was there that she passed away on 3 January 1967. Despite her worldwide fame a mere fifty people turned up at the Aberdeen Crematorium for her funeral.

Over the course of her illustrious career she had earned literally millions of dollars and yet when she died she had some £34 in her handbag and a mere £2 in the bank. Even sadder was the fact that the famous string of pearls had been replaced by an imitation string which was practically valueless. Where all the money had gone James and George Collie, the solicitors attending to her estate, could only speculate but perhaps it is uplifting to suggest that much of it had been spent through the countless acts of generosity for which she was widely recognised and admired.

Several weeks after the funeral the manager of BBC Aberdeen drove to Torphins to visit Mary's sister Helene, who had been unable to attend the funeral as she was incapacitated abroad, and discovered that the lady was tending a bonfire. In response to his enquiry as to what she was burning "Och, these are a lot of letters of Mary's from Debussy. Nobody will be interested in them now."

Sadly, she was correct.

The monument to Mary Garden on Craigie Loanings Aberdeen

Aberdeen's Forgotten Diva is a short musical play by Mike Gibb with music by Mairi (Paton) Warren. It was commissioned by Aberdeen City Council and performed three times on Saturday 27 July 2013 as part of the City's Tartan Day.

It is one woman show and the part of Mary Garden was brilliantly portrayed by local actress and singer Michelle Bruce, who is a distant relation of the opera star, her Mother's maiden name being Garden,

Two of the songs from the show, *Rain on a Flat Tin Roof* and *There Once Was a Time,* were recorded and released on CD.

For further information on the play or the music email mikegibb32@outlook.com.

Annie Murray

(1906-1996)

The Forgotten Heroine of the Forgotten War

On 18 July 1936 the Spanish Civil War began. It was a particularly bloody and distasteful conflict in which an estimated half a million soldiers and civilians died and yet today, less than a hundred years later, it is all but forgotten. This book is not intended to be a history lesson but in order to understand why a wee lassie born in Torphins ended up in a war zone in Spain it is necessary to look back briefly at the events of the 1930's that gave rise to this blight on the sunny Spanish landscape.

In that era Spain was ruled by a democratically elected left wing government who implemented socialist policies that did not please those with conservative and royalist tendencies and, even more importantly, the military and in an effort to curb unrest several leading military chiefs, including General Francisco Franco, were expelled to Morocco where they plotted and waited. Just like Sarajevo two decades earlier, the spark that ignited the flame came in the shape of a political assassination providing Franco with the opportunity to launch an invasion with fellow fascists Hitler in Germany and Mussolini in Italy providing invaluable support including planes to airlift an army of elite troops Franco had assembled in Morocco.

Recruitment poster for the International Brigade

The Spanish government pleaded for help to support their own forces which were in imminent danger of being overrun by Franco's men and their call to arms was heard and answered. Not by the governments of other Western democracies; the British politicians and ruling classes hid behind their Daily Mails and pretended it wasn't happening. No the response came from ordinary men and women.

Many of them were Communists, who arrived from countries around the world to form International Brigades to support Spanish comrades in need.

Countless historians believe that if Britain, France and other European nations had stood up to Franco and his cohorts in 1936 that the scourge of fascism could have been nipped in the bud and the Second World War might have been avoided. Or as John (Patsy) McEwan, a volunteer from Dundee, succinctly put it "If I don't go and fight fascism, I'll just have to wait and fight it here."

Somewhere in the region of fifty thousand volunteers poured into Spain over the course of the three year conflict, travelling from all over Europe, with the largest contingent coming from France, and even from the U.S.A. and beyond. In amongst them were a sprinkling of famous names like writers George Orwell and Ernest Hemingway, actor James Robertson Justice and Willy Brandt, who subsequently became Chancellor of West Germany, but also a lot of just "ordinary folk" including a girl in her thirties born in rural Aberdeenshire.

Annie Murray was the daughter of George Murray, a farmer, and Anne Cargill Murray, and was one of family of eight. Annie was born on the 10th of April 1906 in Newton of Tornaveen, near Torphins and spent her early years there before the family relocated to Glenfarg in Perthshire.

The whole family were staunch socialists and Annie took her political beliefs with her when she headed for Edinburgh Royal Infirmary to train as a nurse. She was less than impressed by the conditions under which the trainee nurses were living and had regular meetings in her room to discuss the situation and try to instigate improvements. She qualified as a nurse in 1936 and having just joined the Communist

Party made the decision to go to Spain because she strongly believed in the cause of the Spanish Republic and was totally opposed to fascism.

Now in the 1930's it wasn't as easy as today to get to Spain; you couldn't just nip along to a Scottish airport, spend three hours in relative comfort consuming over priced food and drink and step off into the sunshine in Alicante or Malaga. In 1936 both the British and French Governments had signed up to the Non-Intervention Agreement which in simple terms meant "who cares about the Spaniards" and individuals were discouraged from travelling. The situation got even more difficult the following year when the British Government dug up some archaic 19th Century piece of legislation making it illegal for anyone to go.

But of course that did not deter those who believed strongly in the cause and felt that it was their duty to help and off they set. The most common route from Scotland began in Glasgow where many volunteers were sent off in groups, cheered on their way by crowds of supporters. It resembled "a Celtic supporters outing" according to one man, who paid, along with many others, the princely sum of £5.00 for the first leg of a bus trip, eventual destination - Hell.

Having arrived in London they waited patiently in Euston Station while money was raised from members of the public with left leaning sympathies to pay for a weekend return tickets to Paris; not that any of them had any intention of using the return ticket to London but by travelling on a tourist train they didn't need a passport, which many didn't possess.

In Paris the volunteers would meet up with others from a variety of countries and a real sense of camaraderie developed. Usually after a pleasant evening in the French capital they were on their way again aboard the "red train" which would take them to the south of France, disembarking in Perpignan and nearby towns close to the Spanish border.

That is when problems sometime arose as there was passport control between the two countries, although many of the local Gendarmes were understanding and supportive and often turned a blind eye to the absence of documentation, The volunteers were then dropped off at the foothills of the Pyrenees and, in silence in case they should alert the many people with fascist tendencies in that area of France, they set off on foot across the mountains, trekking through rough terrain and hiding from searchlights. On average the climb over the mountain range took about eight hours, and then at last they were in Spain, the end of an epic sojourn undertaken not so they could roll up their trouser legs and paddle in the Med but to pick up a rifle and risk their lives on a daily basis.

Annie Murray arrived in Spain in September 1936, just two months into the war, and over the course of the next two and half years worked in a number of hospitals from Huesca in the Aragon region to Huerte in Catalonia and in the city of Barcelona, a stronghold of the Republican movement. Her colleagues in the hospitals often included many other nurses from Britain and a lot of trainee Spanish girls; at that time in Spain there were very few qualified nurses, the work generally being done by nuns, and most of the local girls had only a few months training but Annie found that they were "very keen and very good for the time they had trained."

Annie (centre) with fellow nurses

Annie also discovered that the hospital conditions she encountered were very different from what she had been used to in Scotland and one in particular was somewhat bereft of the levels of cleanliness she had been used it.

A very old building, badly in need of repair. The unit got working together to make it a fit place in which to nurse the wounded. The yard was very dirty and bad-smelling and had to be drained and levelled after many loads of refuse had been removed. We worked at these and other improvements between each attack, so that even if the front was quiet we were always busy.

It is estimated that about 2400 volunteers from Britain travelled to Spain with about 20% of those coming from Scotland. Aberdeen had its own contingent the most famous being Bob Cooney, after whom a street in the Berryden district of the city is now named, while a substantial number came from Dundee, including a man called Tom Clarke who became well known in that city.

Just before Tom set off he was entrusted with a packet of cigarettes to pass to a Communist agent in Paris. Tom was a pipe smoker and during the journey, having run out of pipe tobacco, he thought that they wouldn't miss just one cigarette from a pack of twenty. Unfortunately the one that Tom chose to smoke was the one containing a secret message!

One of the fiercest battle of the war took place in Jarama valley, just south east of Madrid, in early February 1937 and it was there that Tom Clarke was shot in the head. He was tucking into a bowl of rice which suddenly turned red and he realised he had been shot. He survived but surgeons thought it was too dangerous to remove the bullet lodged in his skull and he was sent to a hospital. Later a visiting dentist asked what was wrong with his head and when Tom explained, the dentist took a pair of tweezers and removed the bullet.

Tom was sent to Bennicasim where he stayed in a large coastal villa that had been commandeered and where he successfully recovered. Tom suffered no further mishaps, surviving the rest of the war before returning to Dundee in 1938, and he became a well known figure around the city until he died in his nineties in 2002.

Tom Clarke outside the villa in Bennicasim

Annie treated a wide variety of injuries from the minor to the very severe and as a result encountered some truly horrible and harrowing sights. One of the biggest tasks was treating soldiers who weren't injured by the enemy but were victims of the weather. Spain will normally be thought of us as a warm and sunny country but in the winter, especially in the hills of Catalonia, temperature dropped dramatically and frost bitten feet were a common, serious and very painful complaint.

While working with a Spanish medical group at a large hospital in Barcelona, she was also called upon from time to time to nurse on a hospital train which was a particularly dangerous place to be as they were targets for the German and Italian airplanes sent in support of Franco. Annie recalled that on one occasion they were forced to move the train under a bridge to provide a degree of protection while surgery went on undisturbed.

While Annie devoted her time to nursing the injured and the sick she was in awe of the women who fought on the front line alongside the men and was surprised at just how many women had volunteered. "I think some of them are very brave". Annie also tended soldiers from many different countries with the added complication of the language barrier and even nursed the injured Moors of the invading nationalist army, telling her brother in a letter she had "dealt with a dozen or more who were fascists who were delighted with the treatment they received in our hospital and want to join the government side".

Annie beside a makeshift ambulance

Despite all the horrors that surrounded her – many of the injured arrived with quite appalling injuries – she wrote home that "I would not have liked to miss this experience for anything, gruesome though it is. I have not felt homesick yet." Indeed when she was eventually granted leave she couldn't wait to get back to Spain and to play her part. Although there weren't many lighter moments, at Christmas 1937 she reported that there was a concert and a dance and that she made a Christmas pudding that weighed 200 lbs and which needed four men to lift it into the pot.

In addition to five sisters, Annie had two brothers, Tom and George, both of whom also ended up with the International Brigade. But while the trio of Murrays were in Spain the rest of the family were providing moral support, as well as raising money, back in Scotland. As her sister Margaret said "Anne was in very good spirits and not a bit worried about going out to the fighting zone. Of course, it is much worse for the people left at home isn't it?"

Another sister, Lily, was heavily involved in fund raising in and around Perth, frequently standing up on her soap box and quoting Marxist maxims while a third sister Violet, like Annie also a qualified nurse, received a telegram sent from Spain by Annie saying simply "Come out if possible. Work for you here". But although she was all set to go, the Communist Party, with which she was heavily involved, felt she was too valuable to their efforts to spread the word in London – Violet was by this time nursing in socially deprived Bermondsey – and she was turned down for duty abroad, a decision that her brother Tom approved of.

The remaining three siblings were Agnes and Margaret, both of whom had followed their sisters in nursing, and hairdresser Susan, and all were very supportive of the cause. But Agnes had an infant daughter and Margaret had just got engaged so they stayed home and helped in other ways. There was yet another Murray working tirelessly for the cause in Scotland, Janet who was married to Tom. She was Chairman of the Edinburgh and District Joint Committee for Spanish Relief but while she was giving of her time in Edinburgh her thoughts were often far away in Spain. On one occasion word filtered through that eight Scots had been killed and she spent several apprehensive weeks until she discovered that none of them were members of the Murray clan.

Throughout the period 1936 to 1938 there was a concentrated effort in Britain to provide support in various forms, through fund raising to sending much needed shipments of food, clothing and shoes and it was remarked that in this regard the people of Scotland were particularly generous, thereby expelling a myth perpetrated by our southern neighbours about the miserliness of Scottish people. Fund raising came in a variety of shapes and forms from major events like Spanish Fiestas, street markets and simple bucket collections to a little girl in Bellshill in Glasgow who saved her weekly pocket money, all one half penny of it, to help the children of Spain. But the Murrays and the people of Scotland in general just didn't show their support through the likes of the Spanish Aid Committee.

VICTIMS OF THE CIVIL WAR IN SPAIN

(By kind permission of Planet News, Ltd.)

Refugee Children whose parents perished in an air raid on Madrid.
Thousands of such are now

HOMELESS, HELPLESS & STARVING.

The Scottish Ambulance Unit asks Your immediate help to carry on its humanitarian work. Medical Stores and Food are urgently needed for the wounded and the children.

SUB-COMMITTEE
Bailie Wm. Elger, J P. Sir D. M .Stevenson, Professor Walton.

Please Send Subscriptions to

UNIT SECRETARY, 5 Cleveden Road, Glasgow, W.2.

Ambulance Unit Flag Day 15th May
Collectors Wanted

Name...

Address...

If you wish to help the Spanish People by Collecting,
Post this to the *Unit Secretary*, 5 *Cleveden Road, Glasgow*. W.2,

Printed by the Scotia Press at Crown St. Glasgow C5

45

They also got involved with the Basque Children's Committee who were working to evacuate the children of Guernica. Guernica was a sleepy little town in the North of Spain with a mere 7000 inhabitants back in 1937. It had however huge significance to the Basque peoples of that region as it was their spiritual capital with an oak tree in the central square symbolising freedom for Basques.

Monday 26 April 1937 was a market day in Guernica and as a result people from surrounding areas would have been visiting, swelling the population to about ten thousand. It was while they were doing their shopping in the spring sunshine that the sky was darkened by fleets of bombers from both the German Luftwaffe and the Italian Aviazione. Over the course of four separate waves of attacks they reduced the ancient sleepy town to rubble, with three quarters of all buildings being destroyed, while several hundred civilians are thought to have perished.

The bombing, which was ordered by Franco, was clearly a war crime and yet Western Governments, including the one ensconced in Westminster, merely turned a blind eye to the events. The attack and the effects of the war in the Basque area left close on thirty thousand children homeless or displaced and a worldwide appeal was made for countries to take them as refugees.

France, Russia, Switzerland, Belgium, Denmark and even Mexico agreed to help but not Britain. The British Government was afraid that it might affect the Non-Intervention Treaty and totally refused to get involved with the homeless, and often orphaned, children. But if they thought that was the end of it they hadn't reckoned on the doughty Duchess of Atholl, Katherine Stewart-Murray.

She was a remarkable woman although that is not a view that was widely shared by other members of the aristocracy or in the Scottish Unionist Party (closely associated with the English Conservative and Unionist Party) of which she was not only a member but for whom she served as an MP for Kinross and West Perthshire, becoming the first ever female Scottish MP in the process.

Her disagreement with the Party stemmed largely from her dislike of fascist sympathisers and led to her travelling to Spain in 1937 to see first-hand the effects on Spanish cities of the German and Italian bombing raids. While she was there she also visited captured Republicans held in prisons and was so moved by her experiences that when she returned to Britain she wrote a book *Searchlight on Spain* which clearly displayed her support for the Republican Government and earned her the nickname the "Red Duchess". It also damaged her political career although it was Chamberlain's appeasement of Hitler that so sickened her that she resigned her parliamentary seat.

The Duchess of Atholl

She became the chair of the National Joint Committee for Spanish Relief and later the Basque Children's Committee and toured Scotland raising awareness of the plight of the Spanish people and helping with fund raising in a wide variety of ways.

When Westminster announced its intransigent stance on the Basque refugee children, she managed to stir up a sense of outrage about the despicable bombing and its consequences that support for her campaign to take Basque refuge children here blossomed and eventually the British Government caved in and agreed to accept a single boatload of children and their supportive adults. Even then they made it abundantly clear that the full cost of bringing them and looking after them was to be met by charities and refused to pay a single penny towards the rescue mission.

On the 21st of May 1937 the S.S. Habana left the port of Bilbao headed for Southampton. The ageing vessel was meant to take 800 passengers but as the UK government was only willing to allow "one boatload" of refugees to dock, 3860 children, mainly from Guernica and the neighbouring city of Bilbao, crowded onto the ship along with over 200 adults. It must have been a fairly unpleasant two days for all on board, many of whom were living and sleeping in the lifeboats and any other available space, as they weather was wild in the Bay of Biscay.

S.S. Habana with its four thousand refugees docks at Southampton

They did, however, make it safely to Southampton and the children must have been excited by the scene that greeted their arrival, with the quayside festooned with bunting; they were oblivious to the fact that the flags and other paraphernalia had not been specially displayed for them but were left over from the coronation of George VI ten days earlier. A camp had been prepared for them near Eastleigh where they remained until they were dispersed in small groups around the country.

That is where the Dundee Spanish Aid Committee got involved and began looking for somewhere that could offer refuge to some of the children. A search for suitable accommodation in Dundee proved fruitless but the Dundee Free Breakfast Mission offered the use of a large house known as Mall Park in the seaside town of Montrose. The first children arrived in Montrose in September and were warmly greeted by a group of locals carrying a welcome banner.

The plaque on the building in Montrose where the Basque children stayed in 1937-39

In all 24 children were accommodated in Montrose and although they initially suffered from homesickness they settled in well and generally enjoyed their stay in Scotland, one refugee later describing how they had lived "immensely happily and joyfully". Throughout their stay donations from all over Scotland and from all factions of society poured in and the children repaid the kindness in their own way by providing the entertainment to a huge audience in an event staged in Dundee's Caird Hall. While most of the financial support was raised in traditional ways, the Edinburgh Basque Children's Committee took a more refined approach by holding a garden fete hosted by Lady Salvesen.

The children remained in Montrose for a year until there was suitable accommodation for them back in the Basque country and it was regarded as reasonably safe for them to return to Spain. But they didn't all go back immediately with two of the children staying on in their foster land long after the others had left while it is clear that many years later many of the children retained a great fondness for the people of Montrose and Scotland as a whole.

Although Annie was the first of the Murray clan to venture to Spain she was quickly followed by her younger brother George who became a well known figure in the International Brigades. When he arrived in Spain in 1937 he underwent basic training which lasted between four and six weeks and which, bearing in mind the majority of the men had never seen or held a gun before, was in George Murray's own words "more or less useless".

After being involved in a number of battles and skirmishes George's luck ran out when he was shot and ended up in hospital remarking that he was well looked after by the German doctors and enjoyed far better food than he had on the front line. Unfortunately for Annie there was little information available about what had happened to her brother and it was only after several months of worry and searching at a number of medical facilities that she found him in the hospital in Huete and was delighted to be able to look after him and nurse him back to health.

Like so many other volunteers George found the locals to be "likeable and friendly" and in an effort to be able to converse with them, especially the young senoritas, he attended a Spanish class to learn the language and became such a fluent linguist that he commented that "My Spanish is so perfect that the Spaniards hardly understand a word I am saying!" As soon as he was fit enough George was back on the front line and took part in one of the International Brigades successes, the crossing of the Ebro River, driving back Nationalist forces in the process.

The effect of our advance over the Ebro should be great for it certainly constitutes one of the biggest smashes in the eye that Mussolini and his company ever got and proves the vitality and capacity of the truly magnificent Spanish people. Two years of bitter front line fighting and wanton slaughter in the rear by Italian and

German aviation have failed to destroy not only their spirit but also their resourcefulness and initiative.

George Murray was accompanied at the Ebro offensive by his elder brother Tom, a somewhat later recruit to the cause. Tom was a Councillor in Edinburgh when, in January 1938 he and a dozen volunteers he had persuaded to join him, headed off to Spain. Tom served as Machine Gun Company's Political Commissar and became known by the nick name "Machine Gun Murray". After the success at Ebro Tom wrote home.

We have had the glorious privilege of participating in the remarkable victory of the crossing of Ebro. I am sitting on a hill about 20 metres inside what was until a fortnight ago fascist territory. You may take it that the advance we have made is merely a prelude of more to come, although we are well aware that fascism will throw still more material and men into the struggle in the hope that by doing so this position will be retrieved.

We have no illusions that the victory will be an easy one but on the other hand the recent success confirms with tremendous emphasis the power of the Spanish Republic and sends the morale of all lovers of freedom and justice shooting up to great heights.

The British Battalion of the International Brigade

Tom Murray was correct in his assessment of the nationalist position as they did attack with renewed vigour and the tide turned against the International Brigade. By September 1938 it was becoming clear that Franco's superior forces would prevail but the British Battalion of the International Brigade were asked to undertake one last task prior to repatriation – to go back to the front line to give the Republicans time to reinforce from elsewhere.

They called for volunteers and all the men did so; sadly it turned into a disaster and over the course of three days of fierce fighting at Sierra Lavall over 200 members of the Brigade were killed, wounded or captured. A very sad ending to a campaign of great bravery.

Both of Annie Murray's brothers survived and, following an announcement by the Spanish Prime Minister that all foreign volunteers should return home, thirteen thousand members of the International Brigades marched through Barcelona on 28 October 1938 where they were addressed by a number of high ranking politicians although the words that would remain longest in the minds of the volunteers were those of Dolores Ibarruri.

La Pasionaria statue in Glasgow

Comrades of the International Brigade....you offered your blood...you can go with pride. You are history. You are legend. You are the historic example of the solidarity and the universality of democracy. Come back to us and here you will find a homeland.

Dolores Ibarruri was a renowned fighter for the Republican cause and became better known as La Pasionaria (The Passionflower) whose rallying call "No pasaran" (They shall not pass) became the slogan of the Republican Army. When Franco came to power in 1939 Ibarruri went into exile only returning to her beloved Spain in 1977, two years after the dictator died.

In 1979 a statue of her was erected in Glasgow, on Clyde Street not far from George Square in memory of the 65 members of the International Brigade from that city killed in the conflict. A group of Conservative Party Councillors in Glasgow protested vigorously against the statue claiming that they would "tear in down when they came to power". The statue still stands.

George Murray, like all the others, was amazed at the reception the grateful people of Barcelona afforded them "It was a very emotional sort of thing. Young girls were coming over and kissing you, all this kind of thing, which is surprising after all this time."

A local girl hands a flower to International Brigade soldier

Sadly that was not possible as by February 1939 it was clear that victory for Franco's nationalist forces was inevitable and she was back on a train heading from Barcelona to France. While in Perpignan she visited a friend of the Murray family held in a concentration camp and was successful in negotiating the girl's release before heading back home by a mixture of plane, ferry and train.

 Her experiences had clearly left its mark on her as she explained that she "never want to see anything like it again. Hell is putting it mildly. This has left a black mark on my memory which I shall never be able to throw off". While the horrors of caring for the horribly injured combatants had deeply affected her it was another totally repugnant element of what she coped with that affected her most and left her with terrible memories.

In November 1938 in the final months of the war Annie was confused when there was a sudden intake of children suffering horrific injuries and was totally shocked when she discovered the cause. After years of war many of the children were starving and pounced on chocolate boxes dropped by Italian airplanes.

Sadly when the children eagerly opened them they discovered they were not filled with confectionary but with small bombs which exploded, blowing off their hands and burning their faces. A totally disgusting example of the depth of man's cruelty and inhumanity.

After her return from Spain, Annie settled in London and began work as a nurse in Dulwich Hospital while during the Second World War she volunteered for the Civil Defence Service. Later she became matron of a children's nursery in Stepney.

In 1948 Annie married Frank Knight and worked for the Post Office until her retirement in 1964 when the couple relocated to Cairneyhill near Dunfermline and lived out their remaining days there, both of them dying in 1996. Until the end of her life Annie maintained a great interest in Spain and through the International Brigade Memorial Trust was often seen at anniversaries and memorials. Despite all she saw and all she endured during her time in Spain it was clear that she never regretted it.

It was the most important thing in my life. It was a terrific experience that I would never like to have missed. I have certainly no regrets at having gone there at all.

Annie Murray with brothers Tom (left) and George with the International Brigade banner

Mary Slessor
(1848-1915)

Mother of All the Peoples

In the early hours of 13 January, 1915 in a dingy hut in Use, Calabar the devoted adopted family of an elderly and terminally ill lady gathered around her bed and heard her whisper in the native Efik language "Oh God release me". As dawn broke, her wish was granted. This story begins, however, 67 years earlier and three thousand miles away in Aberdeen in a run-down granite building on what was then known as Mutton Brae, now part of the Denburn dual carriageway, where on the 2 of December 1848 Mary Mitchell Slessor entered this world.

Mary was one of seven children although sadly three of those died during their early years. Despite these tragedies the Slessor family were devout Christians and regular attendees at the United Presbyterian Church on Belmont Street. The building subsequently became the school hall for the Central School/ Aberdeen Academy and is now part of the Academy Shopping Centre and there is a plaque on the side of the building, rather strangely positioned above a cash dispensing machine, to record that Mary regularly worshipped there.

Plaque on Belmont Street Aberdeen

Her father hailed from the Buchan area and her mother from Kirk Street, Oldmeldrum and during her early years Mary regularly stayed with her grandparents in Oldmeldrum. Her association with the town is commemorated by the naming of a street Mary Slessor Place. Her mother was a sweet and docile person with infinite patience. It could be argued that she was fortunate with her husband as he gave her plenty of practice at being patient.

Mary was born into a depressed world during what was known as the 'hungry forties", an era when people fled from the country to the town searching for food and ended up starving and dying on the streets of Aberdeen. Robert Slessor had two occupations, a shoemaker and a drunk but sadly only excelled at one. When he was sober he was a kind and gentle man who doted on Mary but the loss of three children in as many years through the dreaded consumption changed him and drove him to find solace in the bottom of a glass. By the time that Mary had reached the age of ten, Robert had traded his shoemakers' business for whisky and as they couldn't live on the mother's meagre wages as a weaver, they decided to move to Dundee, a city booming on the back of the jute mills.

Baxter Bros. Mill, Dundee

They were told that it was a land of milk and honey and that the streets were paved with gold. They soon discovered that they weren't even paved. Having sold most of their few possessions to pay for the fares the Slessor clan headed south and before Mary knew it she was working at Baxter Brothers Mill as a 'half timer'.

That meant that she spent half the day working in the mill and the other half at school. After she had worked for five hours, having started at 6 am, it was sometimes difficult to concentrate on the school lessons but a leather belt over her knuckles or her knees, if she happened to doze off, certainly helped.

And then came the day when she reached the grand old age of fourteen and could be classed as a woman, able to leave school and go full time to the mill. Her father couldn't wait to see her working extra hours to help finance his quest to drink Dundee dry and so Mary joined thousands of others working for fifty eight hours a week.

The mills were desperate places, dusty and dirty, full of desperate souls working side by side amidst the gloom and the noise. The owners packed the mills with women, who were paid half a man's wage, and children, who could be employed for a quarter of the rate. And pity the young lad as the day he reached manhood would be the very day he would be shown the door to join the ranks of the 'kettle bilers'.

Life in Dundee wasn't quite as Mary had imagined it, with the family living in what was called a single end, a fancy for one room. No gas lights, no running water and no toilet, just one room with a few sticks of furniture: a double bed for mother and father and straw mattresses on the floor for the rest of them. And, of course, the family pail for 'bodily functions' which was emptied onto a communal midden alongside the pails of fifty other families living in the same squalor. The children took it in turns to do the emptying and Mary used to dread it when her turn came round. Years later she could still smell the stench and see the cloud of flies rising as the contents were deposited. They also had a big zinc bath and they would all have a bath using the same lukewarm water once a month, whether they needed it or not.

When her sister Janie arrived there were six of them living in that one room but they were far from alone. At that time 30,000 folk were living in same foul conditions in Dundee. But despite the privation, the first few months were bliss for Mary. Her father was off the drink and there was enough money coming into keep them all fed. Sadly it proved to be a false dawn as before long Robert was back to his old ways and Mary's mother would spend Saturday nights waiting for him to come home in the hope that he hadn't spent all their money in the pub.

And when he didn't appear Mary would be despatched to go round the pubs to try and find him. In no time at all Mary became acquainted with all the bars in the area. The John O' Groats on the Cowgate, the Pillars and the Old Bank Bar on the Murraygate, Mickey Coyle's and half a dozen others beside. She hated going into these places as they were full of drunken men with beery breaths and wandering hands.

On the nights that she was unable to find her father she returned home somewhat distraught but knowing that her work was not yet done and her Mother would be looking for her to carry out one more task, that of "going doon the road". Her mother still had some pride and could never bring herself to say the word "pawnbroker" and so with a parcel hidden under her shawl so that the neighbours didn't know what she was up to Mary, would head for the pawnbrokers shop. Mind you on occasions the items didn't take much hiding as a wedding ring, the only item of jeweller her mother owned, would slip easily in her pocket and the few pennies she would collect would keep the family fed for a wee while longer.

As a result of her experience of going round the pubs in Dundee she came to the conclusion that there were two kinds of drunks. There was the good natured ones who called everybody pal and ended up singing melancholy songs usually extolling the virtues of Scotland. On the other hand there were those always looking for a fight and unfortunately Robert Slessor fell into that latter category.

For that reason she began to dread Saturday nights and the creak on the stairs to announce that her father was coming home. In his drunken state he would always find something to blame his wife for - the fact that his tea wasn't ready or that it was burnt because he was late - and his reaction was always the same as he lashed out at Mary's mother. Mary was small but she was red haired with a fiery temper and she would often end up with a black eye or a bloody nose through trying to defend her mother and find herself thrown out of the house, left to sit and shiver on the dark stairs until her father had fallen asleep in a drunken stupor.

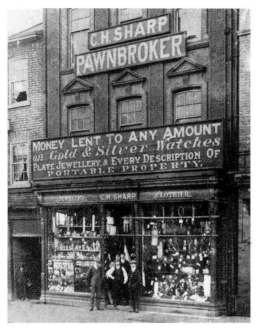

Dundee 19ᵗʰ Century Pawnbroker

When her father died Mary didn't grieve a great deal and following his death the family moved up in the world a little to a new house. It was still a slum but a better class of slum.

In her early years Mary was known locally as "carrots" or sometimes "fire" because of the colour of her hair and her famous temper and it is fair to say that she was hardly an angel back then. But one day that all changed. Mary and a few of her chums had taken to visiting Mrs Walker, a widow woman that stayed nearby, going there simply because she always had a roaring fire in the grate and would give them a cup of tea and a bannock if they would listen to her sermons on hell and damnation. One night when Mrs Walker was going on with one of her lectures about repenting and so on, the girls were capering about and paying little attention to what she was saying. Suddenly Mrs Walker grabbed Mary's hand and it looked as if she was going to put it into the fire. Mary struggled to get free but the woman was too strong for her and she said "if you were to put your hand in there it would be awful sore wouldn't it? Well if you don't repent you're soul will burn in blazing fires forever".

Mary didn't think much about it at the time but then she started to have nightmares where an old crone would appear and try and force her into a blazing fire. As a consequence Mary began to reflect on life and God and started to read her Bible, really understanding it for the first time. It changed her life as she realised that she could speak to God and decided that she was going to dedicate her life to doing his work.

She explored the possibility of becoming a missionary but it was clear that the Mission Board didn't look for young lassies coming from her background, living in the slums of Dundee. But her mother suggested that she go and speak to the Reverend Logie at the local church to see if he needed any help and as volunteers in church circles are a bit of rarity, the minister welcomed her with open arms. He asked her to help with the Sunday school and also in setting up a mission in Queen Street right in the heart of the slums.

Mary threw herself into both tasks and delighted in taking some of the slum kids, who had never seen the countryside, up the hills where they would have picnics and play games. While the minister was delighted with this initiative, some of the elders were not so pleased and the minister ended up faced with a deputation of elders complaining about "thon terrible Slessor lassie who's leading the bairns astray, encouraging them to run races up and doon the hills and even climb trees". The minister said that he would look into it but was well aware of the good that Mary was doing and did little if anything to discourage it. He called Mary his "recruiting sergent" as she had been able to persuade so many people to come to the mission. The very fact that she loved going wasn't enough for Mary as in her mind everyone should do the same and before long she became known for miles around and people would cross the street just to avoid a session of her preaching.

There was a famous summer's night when she spotted these four young lads hanging about a street corner while she was on the way to the mission. Like a magnet she was attracted to them and quickly began her usual spiel. The leader of the wee gang was twirling a big lead weight on a length of rope and began swinging it around his head in her general direction trying to scare her. She decided to do a deal with them; if she could stand there without drawing back they would all have to come to the mission with her.

The boy with the rope began to let out more and more until the weight got closer and closer to her head. She couldn't let on that she was scared and tried to appear nonchalant or as nonchalant as she could with two pound of lead heading in her direction. She did however take off her good Sunday hat just in case the thing hit her. The game went on until the lead was about 3 inches from her face when the lad said "she's game boys" and let it drop and like a troop of little angels they followed her to the mission. That lad not only became a regular at the mission but a good friend of Mary's throughout her life.

Every Sunday morning the whole family would dress in their "Sunday Best" for despite the fact that they didn't have twa maiks to rub together they had to have on their Sunday outfits which only saw the light of day on the Sabbath or when a missionary came to town. Mary's mother had an obsession with missionaries and was ever hopeful that her son John would take up the calling.

When her brother John sadly succumbed to the TB just a few short months after he had been sent to New Zealand for his health Mary suggested that she could be the member of the Slessor family that heeded the call. Her mother pointed out that she had two major disadvantages - she wasn't educated and she was a woman.

There was nothing she could do about the later but she set about overcoming the other obstacle.

She took to reading *The Missionary Record* and became totally fascinated with the work of one Scottish lad, David Livingstone learning that Livingstone had been a mill worker from Blantyre who educated himself by reading books while working the loom. She decided to try to do the same and for the next few years she read, no devoured every book she could lay her hands on and especially every word she could find about David Livingstone, fascinating tales of his travels to darkest Africa spreading the Christian message.

She was 25 when she heard that Livingstone had died in the African bush and she was devastated and felt like she had lost one of her family. But one day a few months later an idea began to form in her head; she would follow in David Livingstone's footsteps and go to Africa, to Calabar, a part of Nigeria that she had read about. It sounded so mysterious although her sister Susan was not impressed by Mary's intentions, pointing out what a dreadful place Calabar was and how it had gained a reputation as the "white man's grave".

A young Mary dressed in her missionary finery

Undeterred Mary discussed this madcap idea with the minister and after working extra hard educating herself she wrote to the Foreign Missionaries Board. She was shaking so much that she could hardly open the letter of reply when it came but there it was in black and white - "Mary Mitchell Slessor is invited to go to Calabar as a missionary". She was ecstatic right until the very night before she was due to leave home.

Not that she was heading for darkest Africa the next day, only darkest Edinburgh to attend college for four months but for a lassie that had never been beyond the Sidlaw hills, Edinburgh seemed far away. And for a lassie that had spent every night of her life for the previous twenty eight years under the same roof as her mother, four months seemed like forever.

She sat on the tenement stairs and cried her eyes out. The minister came round and tried to reason with her but it was impossible and just as he left Mary shouted to him, "Pray for me. Please pray for me." It was a desperate plea from someone with a broken heart. That night she would have done anything to avoid leaving the next day but she went and quickly settled into life and in auld reekie and weeks flew by. On reflection she came to the conclusion that she wasn't sure how much she learned and suggested that a couple of weeks apprenticed to a builder would have been of far more practical benefit to her in Africa.

But her spell in Edinburgh got her used to life away from home and it gave her the opportunity to mix with people who were equally determined to take up the calling, reassuring her that she was doing the right thing. So by the time that August came round and she was set to leave she felt like a real missionary and one that was ready for the great adventure.

When David Livingstone died Mary cut out a newspaper article quoting words he had written shortly before his death and she referred to it from time to time. It said "I direct your attention to Africa. I know that in a few years I shall be cut off in that country which is now open. Do not let it be shut again. Carry out the work I have begun. I leave it to you." If she needed any further encouragement to pack her case and follow in his footsteps that article provided it.

On the 5th of August 1876 Mary bade a long and tearful farewell to her mother and her sisters in Dundee railway station before setting off on the first leg of her journey by train to Liverpool. Two friends accompanied her to see her safely settled on the ship. The S.S. Ethiopia, tied up at the quayside, was quite a sight, the biggest ship she had ever seen and as she approached it she noticed they were loading hundreds and hundreds of casks of rum but "only the one missionary".

The ship sailed the next day and Mary was by the rail as it left the quayside. She waved and waved at her friends until they were no more than specks in the distance and couldn't possibly see her. At last she was on her way.

The S. S. Ethiopia

Mary spent much of the voyage in her cabin reading and preparing herself for the task ahead and quickly found her sea legs which was just as well as when they reached the Bay of Biscay they ran into a storm. A young officer found her on deck and assumed that she was afraid. She wasn't in fact but wanted to experience the ferocity of the storm first-hand. He asked her if she was scared that the ship would sink. "Na na laddie" she replied "God widnae send me all this way just to drown me on your silly auld ship".

And then at last, after more than two months at sea, she was there and as the ship neared the shore she caught sight of Calabar and smelt the palm oil wafting on the warm breeze. It was just as she had always imagined it and she could barely control her excitement as they moved up the Cross River and berthed at Duke Town. And then suddenly it hit her. She had travelled 3000 miles to the other side of the world. She was 3000 miles from her mother and her sister and her friends. 3000 miles from her home.

Mary initially found herself staying in a large house with a number of other missionaries all of whom were beautifully dressed and lived a pampered and privileged life in comparison with the natives who survived in conditions that made the slums of Dundee look luxurious. It was not a situation that pleased Mary and in an effort to understand them better Mary decided to spend a night in one of the native villages.

It proved to be quite an experience as she slept in a hut that was overrun with rats and cockroaches with six local women for company. And in effort to make Mary feel welcome they insisted in sleeping close to her in a manner that reminded Mary of "sardines", albeit rather large and rather sweaty sardines.

She was also shocked and horrified by some of the local customs no more so than when she witnessed the burial of a local chief. Clearly feminism hadn't reached Calabar as the dead chief's wives, and he had several, were now regarded as worthless and were dragged kicking and screaming to the grave side. And then they were thrown into the pit with the body and buried alive. She later recalled that she couldn't get the sound of their pleading and screaming out of her head for a long time.

The native women were normally rather large as that was what the local men desired and Mary was both bemused and amused by the fattening houses, huts where girls of marrying age were kept and regularly fed on the richest food until they were big enough to be regarded as suitable for a wife. Considerably less humorous was the method of ascertaining the innocence or guilt of someone charged with a crime. This was not established by court proceeding but simply by forcing the accused to swallow a potion that included esere, a local bean that was poisonous. If the person vomited up the potion, an unusual outcome, it displayed their innocence; if they didn't and they died, well that just showed that they had been guilty all along. Justice was done, Calabar style.

During her early days in Africa she also encountered the strange and unsettling tradition regarding the arrival of twins. The natives were highly superstitious and looked on twins as unnatural, believing that one of them must have been sired by the devil and as they couldn't tell which of the twins it was, both were killed at birth.

But it wasn't only these practices that caused Mary distress; there was also malaria. At that time no one had established that the disease was carried by mosquitoes, an insect that thrived in the damp, swamp like conditions of Calabar, and Mary regularly suffered bouts of the debilitating disease, greatly affecting her health and well being. She was also homesick, desperately missing her mother and her sisters. The Missionary Board recognised that she was weak and drained and depressed and shipped her home a year before she was due a spell of leave.

She arrived back in Dundee somewhat deflated, considering herself a failure, and with little desire to return. She poured out her heart to her family admitting that she felt like a fish out of water living in the big fancy house and wearing facing clothes and that she didn't get nearly enough time with the natives that she had gone to help.

Much as she enjoyed being back with her family, especially as she was now financially capable of helping them to move to a better and healthier living environment in Downfield on the outskirts of Dundee, one element of life back in Scotland didn't thrill her. The lectures. All returning missionaries were expected to travel around Scotland giving talks about life in Africa in order to raise funds and hopefully to encourage others to follow in their footsteps.

The problem was that Mary was very conscious of her absence of a formal education and found it especially difficult to speak to groups where there was an abundance of men, her experiences with her abusive father leaving her permanently wary of the sex. However she carried out this duty as best she could and reaped the rewards many years later as a result of a talk she gave in Falkirk where amongst the audience were two young girls called Janet Wright and Martha Peacock, both of whom ended up working with her in Calabar.

Despite their reluctance to lose her again her mother and sister accepted that Mary was born to be a missionary and slowly rebuilt her self esteem and quashed her desire to give it all up. Mary emerged from her depressed state and vowed to go back but only if she could do it on her own terms.

Mary spent a year in Dundee before returning to Calabar having convinced the Missionary Board that she could do far more good away from the big house in Duke Town and on her return she was sent to Old Town where she had the opportunity to establish schools, churches and a dispensary both in Old Town itself and in outlying areas, as a result of which she earned the respect, friendship and support of King Eyo.

Shortly before she was due to take her second spell of leave and return to Dundee she rescued yet another set of twins but on this occasion their parents discovered where the babies were and managed to find the boy child and kill him. For several days Mary stood vigil over the little girl until, and despite suffering from yet another bout of malaria, she was able to get on a ship with the child and head for Scotland.

Her arrival was greeted by her mother and sisters with a mixture of joy and disbelief, seeing the lassie from Dundee cradling a little black bundle, and the puzzled look on their faces caused Mary to burst out laughing. She called the wee one Jean Annan Slessor, named after her sister Janie, and the baby was baptised at the Wishart Memorial Sunday School.

While at home Mary was again required to do the lecture tour but this time round it proved much easier as the gatherings had less interest in what Mary had to say than in the little girl as few if any of those attending would ever have seen a black baby, or any coloured person, before. As a consequence interest in and financial support for the Missionary Board and their work increased dramatically.

While Mary enjoyed being back in Dundee she became increasingly concerned by the health of her sister Janie who was diagnosed with TB or consumption as it was called in the 19th Century. When her mother also developed symptoms Mary found a house for rent in the warmer and drier climate of Devon and they all moved there with the exception of her other sister Susan.

The change of air appeared to agree with them, their health improved and they settled into the community of Topsham near Exeter. But just when things were looking up for the Slessor clan came the news that Susan had died quite suddenly while visiting friends in Edinburgh. When shortly afterwards the health of Mary's mother deteriorated, Mary tendered her resignation to the Missionary Board, concluding that she was needed more at home than abroad. However, her mother did not agree with this decision telling her daughter "You are my child given to me by God and I have given you back to him". After much soul searching Mary resumed her vocation and in November 1885 set sail once again for Calabar, knowing in her heart of hearts that it was unlikely that she would ever see her mother or sister again.

Mary with Jean (Janie)

Female missionaries had always been beautifully turned out in pristine uniforms topped off with bonnets and lacy gloves but Mary decided that if she was going to fit in she couldn't go about looking like a porcelain doll. And so she got rid of all the finery including the layers and layers of underskirts and the shiny shoes and produced the Mary Slessor uniform for the African jungle. It comprised of a petticoat and...well actually it comprised of just a petticoat and bare feet.

It was not terribly ladylike or deemed suitable but it was certainly practical in Mary's case. Unfortunately the Missionary Board got wind of it and sent a Mission visitor to ask Miss Slessor to conform. By this time Mary was well established and had gained in confidence due to the success of the various initiatives she had put in place and as a result the woman was sent away with a flea in her ear and Mary carried still "unsuitably" dressed.

Back in Old Town she resumed her work under the auspices of King Eyo, a converted Christian with remarkably only one wife. But that still wasn't enough for Mary who wanted to go and live amongst the Okoyong tribe despite the fearsome reputation that they had. She raised this idea with the Board and was told that "the Okoyongs are little better than savages, uneducated and uncivilised" to which Mary responded "Isn't that the very reason we should be going to live among them?" The Board members all considered that she was mad but nevertheless she was given the necessary permission.

On her first visit to the Okoyongs she was totally on her own, the canoe party, reluctantly provided by King Eyo who had warned her about the potential dangers, dropping her off and quickly heading to the far side of the Cross River, terrified of their rival tribe. Mary undaunted walked the four miles through the jungle until she came upon their village and met with the formidable Chief Edem who must have been impressed by the courage of the small white woman and agreed that she could come and live with them and teach them "book" as they called education.

As a result several weeks later Mary moved all of her possessions and five children including Janie (Jean), to the land of the Okoyong and began teaching. She set up a dispensary where she was able to cure a few minor ailments with the meagre supply of drugs she had access to and established an open-air church where she would get the natives to sing hymns set to old Scots tunes. After the service she loved to examine the contents of the collection plate which could yield up items as diverse as snuff boxes, fishing hooks, brass rods and many other weird and wonderful things.

Mary amongst the Okoyong people

Mary also loved to see some of the native women coming along dressed in a strange mixture of second hand clothes donated by the people of Scotland including a few items which she was sure the original owners must have been happy to see the back of and would never cease to marvel at these women who would normally wear very little, or even less, all dressed up in this manner, carrying on the "Sunday Best" tradition.

While she worked tirelessly to help the Okoyong people, her thoughts were never far from her family now living in England and she was delighted when a letter arrived to impart the news that both her mother and her sister were well. Sadly three days after the letter had been posted her mother succumbed to consumption and three months later her sister Janie also died. This left Mary as the only surviving member of the Slessor family despite the fact that she had lived for many years in what was regarded as one of the unhealthiest countries in the world.

Over the next decade Mary's workload steadily increased leaving no time for romance but that all changed when a young recruit to the missionary service, Charles Morrison, arrived on the scene. Their initial meeting was in the Mission House in Duke Town and Charles visited her when a particularly severe attack of malaria meant that Mary was hospitalised. They quickly discovered that they both loved books and shared a sense of humour and before long and despite the age difference (Mary was by this time 42 and Charles 24) he proposed to her and Mary accepted. Charles provided a ring although she seldom had occasion to wear it as it was unlikely that the local chief would ask "can I see your ring Mary. Oh it's lovely".

To get married they required the approval of the Missionary Board and they approached them for permission. It isn't clear why they frowned upon two of their missionaries getting married but they would not give Charles Morrison consent to move permanently to Ekenge where Mary was by then settled which meant that Mary would have to move if the couple were to be together. After much soul searching Mary concluded that this was not something she could do as she had become very attached to the Okoyong people.

I could not leave my work for such a reason. To leave a field like Okoyong without a worker and to go to ten or a dozen where the people have an open Bible and plenty of privilege! It is absurd! If God does not send him up here he must do his work and I must do mine where we have been placed.

So the marriage was off and because of ill health Charles Morrison was sent back to Kikintilloch in Dunbartonshire. He never returned to Africa, moving instead to North Carolina where he died at a young age. It is clear from a letter that Mary wrote to his mother after his death how much she had cared for Charles and throughout her life she was never without two books, *Eugene Aram* and *Sketches by Boz* (Charles Dickens first published work) that he had given her as a gift.

After years of promises Chief Edem had at last built her a house of her own. Until then she lived in a small hut next to the Chief's harem which was not only uncomfortable but embarrassing as the walls were very thin and visiting Chiefs and dignitaries of other tribes were allowed unfettered access to the harem women. Mary moved the few bits and pieces of furniture and other items she had collected over the years into her new abode. She had quickly adapted to the basics of life in Ekenge and she overcame the lack of material goods, which people in Scotland took for granted, in often inventive ways.

In the absence of an alarm clock to wake her in the mornings she got hold of a cockerel and tied him up alongside her bed. And regular as any clock it woke her at dawn every day and she didn't even need to worry about remembering to set it before she went to bed.

Adjacent to this new house was a Church which doubled as a school and both were well attended. Gradually over the years the locals began to accept and respect her although the local witch doctor was never impressed, no doubt considering Mary and her medicines a threat to his power and he never quite forgave her for embarrassing him in front of the natives.

It all began when Mary heard a commotion outside her hut and went to investigate, discovering a lassie staked out naked on the ground with a group of warriors dressed in all their finery dancing around her and with the witchdoctor swinging a large ladle. Alongside him stood a cauldron of oil bubbling away and Mary discovered that the girl had given food to a slave while her husband was not at home and this was construed as adultery, a crime punishable by having boiling oil poured over her stomach.

The famous fiery temper surfaced and Mary stood in front of the witchdoctor, blocking his path to the girl. Playing to the crowd he began advancing towards Mary, swinging the ladle, and expecting Mary to take flight. But she had stood up to the bullies in the streets of Dundee and she wasn't scared of him, So instead of backing away, she stared him down and he was so surprised that he dropped his ladle and ran off. All who witnessed this event, a large crowd including Chief Edem himself had gathered to watch the punishment being carried out, were astounded concluding that such a display of strength from a small white woman clearly showed the power of her God.

Mission House in Ekenge

But such events were fairly commonplace in Mary's life and she regularly had to intervene when innocent people were in danger of torture and death not because of anything they had done but simply as a result of some misfortune having befallen the Chief or his family, the highly superstitious people believing that evil spirits could only be quelled by sacrifices. Mind you it didn't help that the Okoyong people were very heavy drinkers and drunkenness reduced any limited sense of reason they may have possessed.

From time to time the Missionary Board would send out assistants but usually a couple of weeks with Mary, and her extremely basic living conditions, were enough for them and they left. So Mary decided to take matters into her own hands and to place an advert in the Missionary Record.

Needed. Consecrated women who are not afraid of work or filth of any kind moral or material. Women who can wash a baby or teach a child to wash and comb as well as read and write. Women who can take it all to Jesus and there get strength to pull on, under any circumstances. If they play Beethoven and paint and draw and speak French and German so much the better but we can do without these later accomplishments if they have a loving heart, willing hands and commonsense. They will not need fine English for there is none to admire it. I would gladly welcome any warm hearted woman from any sphere if she would come to me.

No one replied and as the workload grew heavier Mary grew weaker. Eventually after fifteen years without a permanent missionary helper, and two years after the Board had told her that she would be coming, Janet Wright arrived.

Janet, a young girl inspired by a talk by Mary in Falkirk many years earlier, had already spent seven years working in Duke Town and Creek Town and knew the native language. She took over the Akpap School and dispensary and helped lighten Mary's burden in so many ways. Mary, who was never known to be overly effusive in her praise of people, wrote about Janet "she is right sisterly helpmate and a help and comfort in every way. I don't know how I got on alone. It seems too good to be true".

Not that Mary, even with a helper, slowed down. If she heard of twins being born anywhere in the area she was off, often walking for hours through the densest jungle, praying that she would be there before the babies were sacrificed. When she did, and she could persuade the locals to comply, she would take the twins home with her and bring them up as her adopted children.

To this day there are many, many people alive who are the direct descendants of babies that Mary rescued and these include Francis Ida Udom, a Nigerian student studying in Scotland, the great grandson of a girl that Mary rescued and named Annie. Several years ago Francis attended a Civic Reception hosted by the local council in the Town Hall in Aberdeen following the unveiling of the memorial to Mary in Union Terrace Gardens.

Mary with some of her adopted family

With no family left alive in Scotland Mary had no great wish to take her next spell of leave and it was delayed even further when a severe outbreak of small pox decimated the community and despite an urgent vaccination program many of the people she had grown close to, including Chief Edem, died. Eventually Mary did head back to Scotland taking four of her adopted children with her and she caused quite a stir when she stepped off a train in Waverly Station in Edinburgh accompanied by the row of little black faces.

Despite her advancing years and regular bouts of illness Mary continued relentlessly with her work, helped as always by Janet Wright, and by 1902 there were no less than four places along the Creek River where schools and churches were in the process of being built. Mary's restlessness to keep spreading the word and setting up new facilities meant there were many emotional farewells when "Ma", as she was known throughout Calabar, moved on to pastures new. Her adopted son Dan summed up Mary leaving Akpap, where she was greatly admired and loved.

It was a most pathetic morning; wailing rent the air, you cannot imagine a whole people so stricken and distressed. Swarms of them came from distant villages with all sorts of presents including yams, plantains, goats, chicken and eggs...as the launch moved off...the great wail went up like thunder, men and women weeping. Ma stood on the upper deck, waving emotionally and as the launch turned the bend she collapsed into a chair.

When it came to building new facilities Mary, as always, was right in the front line. She discovered that the mission house at one of the villages, Itu, had not been completed so she rolled up her sleeves, of a petticoat no doubt, and got to work laying a concrete floor to keep the dreaded driver ants out. Other missionary workers were amazed at her expertise and asked who had taught her.

Naebody. I just mix it and stir it like porridge. Then I turn it oot, smooth it wi' a stick and say "Lord here's is the cement. If it be thy will please set it". And he aye does.

As her fame spread throughout the region she was asked to be Vice President of the Native Council, the first woman to be appointed a magistrate anywhere in the British Empire, and she sat in on every single dispute that arose and gave her judgement. While Mary tried to be scrupulously fair she did ensure that the native women, who were legally regarded as chattels owned by their husbands, emerged as winners. Long before the word was in common use Mary was clearly a feminist as is displayed by a note in her famous Bible, which is on display in Dundee's McManus Galleries. Every square inch is covered with Mary's notes and scribbles and on the page where St Paul spoke about the rights of women in a manner with which Mary did not agree, she added "Na! Na! Paul laddie! This will no do!"

Another major event during her later years in Calabar was the opening of the Mary Slessor Memorial Hospital, which remains operational to this day, and Mary was thrilled when she was asked to preside at the event although in general she really didn't care for pomp and was subsequently extremely reluctant to leave her home to attend an awards ceremony in Duke Town.

The ceremony was to recognise all Mary's work for which she was made an Associate of the Order of St John of Jerusalem, an order approved by King George V. After some persuasion by Janet Wright, she did travel to Duke Town to accept the medal and even got dolled up in "posh clothes" although in typical Mary Slessor fashion she refused to wear dress shoes, as they hurt her feet, and as result is probably the only person to accept a King's silver cross wearing a pair of canvas sand shoes.

When in 1914 the First World War broke out Mary was horrified by the carnage and all the young lads being slaughtered every day on the fields of France, sent to their certain death by politicians who had the gall to describe the people in Africa as "savages". By this time the frequent bouts of malaria, and several other exotic diseases she suffered from, had left Mary weak and infirm but yet determined to carry on her work meaning that on occasions she had to be carried around on a stretcher by four big strong lads. She also insisted on attending church every Sunday and in one of her last letters recalled the joy she derived from her grand children.

Annie's wee girl (Susie) is the sweetest pet and imitates everything and everybody. She runs about in church and will point to me during the service and call to me and yet I CAN'T say don't bring her. There should be room in my Father's House for even the babies.

When 1915 dawned Mary had to face up to her frailty as her life was slipping away and she died in the early hours of 13 January, surrounded by her adopted family and with missionary helper Martha Peacock by her side.

Mary Slessor was sixty seven and had spent over thirty years of her life in Calabar, most of it living in the dense forests amongst natives who became her closest friends. Within hours, news of her death was spread the length and breadth of Calabar by the messenger boys and the jungle drums and the mourning began. On the day of her funeral flags flew at half-mast on all the government buildings in Duke Town, which was hushed and still, and thousands lined the route as her coffin was carried up the Old Mission Road.

Mary was buried in a simple grave and as she was laid to rest the crowds heard her great friend Mammy Fuller utter one word. "Safe". While a few women cried quietly there was none of the weeping and wailing common at African funerals. The natives stood in silence, their heads bowed, displaying a quiet dignity. It was a final and touching tribute to Ma. The Mother of All the Peoples.

Granite cross and plaque marking Mary's grave

The final word on Mary's remarkable story should perhaps be given to the British High Commissioner for the area, in an article for the London Morning Post where he wrote '*She, Miss Slessor, can go where no white man can go. She can sway people where we cannot sway them.*'

Remembering Mary

In her city of birth there is scant recognition of one of its most famous daughters and indeed for many years it comprised of nothing more than the plaque on Belmont Street, paid for by the Rotary Club.

The Mary Slessor Foundation were determined to help rectify that situation although it took a lot of telephone calls, emails and arm twisting before a proper memorial was commissioned. After judging three maquettes by sculptors a decision was made to go with the work of Mary Bourne who came with the inventive idea of creating a granite bowl of material sourced from Kemnay quarry in the shape of the water pots made by hand by Nigerian women, with an infill of a bronze replica of a native African flower. We asked for it to be sited in Union Terrace gardens as close as possible to where the house Mary had been born into had once stood and a plaque providing a brief history of Mary's remarkable life was added.

Mary Slessor Monument Union Terrace Gardens

Her adopted city of Dundee has gone quite a bit further. There is permanent exhibition at the McManus Galleries which also boasts a truly wonderful double stained glass window, one side depicting Mary at work in the Dundee mills, the other Mary in Africa. It is worth a visit, especially on a sunny day when the sun shines through it.

In January 2015, the hundredth anniversary of her death, a new memorial to Mary was unveiled outside the city's Steeple Church while in even more recent times, as part of the waterfront redevelopment, a large square was created between the Caird Hall and the V. & A. Museum. This square now regularly hosts large scale outdoor concerts and musical events and is known as Slessor Gardens.

Mary is also remembered in her adopted home of Calabar. A large cross of granite imported from Aberdeen marks the site of her grave in Duke Town; her great friend and fellow missionary Charles Ovens on seeing it commented "It'll tak' mair than that tae hold doon our Mary". There are also various statues and other tributes around the country and the women of the Church's Guild wear a colourful outfit with a large portrait of Mary on the front.

Over the course of the last two decades the Mary Slessor Foundation, run by Dr Lawrie Mitchell (who received a MBE for his work) and his wife Eme (the great granddaughter of Chief Edem's sister), have transformed the area of Akpap Okoyong by building a Skills Training Centre, an Agricultural Processing Unit, a Clinic and more.

And of course in addition, if you come across a Clydesdale £10 from the decade 1997/2006 you will see Mary's face on the front and a map on the back. Its issue made Mary the first woman, other than the Queen, ever to appear on a Scottish bank note.

The stage play *Mother of All the Peoples,* with music by Mairi Paton, debuted at the Lemon Tree Aberdeen in early 2003 directed by Annie Inglis and, having sold out its run a month before opening night, enjoyed another sell out run at the larger Aberdeen Arts Centre in November of that same year. The cast of Jill Hay, Yvonne Morton and Sarah Alexander, reprised their roles on several other occasions in subsequent years as well as recording the music which was released as an original cast CD.

Following its success in Aberdeen, a production was staged at the Gardyne Theatre in Dundee, directed by John Nimmo, and on the strength of that was invited to transfer to firstly the Byre Theatre in St Andrews and subsequently the prestigious Dundee Rep. Following an early cast change, four actresses – Lynne Binnie, Tricia Stewart, Aileen Air and Carolyn Johnston – performed the play regularly for the next ten years in the likes of the Gardyne Theatre and again at the Dundee REP as well as Mitchell Hall in Glasgow.

Mother of All the Peoples was also presented in an abridged form in the new Scottish Parliament building at Holyrood, the first musical ever to be performed there. The most recent production (at the time of writing anyway) was in Dundee in 2015 as part of the commemoration of 100 years since Mary died and a new cast CD with a slightly expanded score was released. Over the course of the period from 2005 to 2015 the musical play, thanks to the generosity of the casts and crew, raised tens of thousands of pounds for the Mary Slessor Foundation.

For further information on the musical play, which is now licensed for amateur productions, or the music contact mikegibb32@outlook.com

Maria Ogilvie-Gordon
(1864-1939)

The "Firsts" Lady

"Never in the field of human endeavour has one woman achieved so many firsts but been known by so few". Apologies to Winston Churchill for paraphrasing his famous speech.

The "Firsts" lady in question was Maria Matilda Ogilvie, although often referred to as May, born in the lovely Aberdeenshire village of Monymusk on 30 April 1864. Her parents were Maria Ogilvie and her husband the Reverend Alexander Ogilvie who at the time of her birth taught at Monymusk School before becoming the headmaster of Robert Gordon's Hospital (subsequently Robert Gordon's College).

Despite the title, Robert Gordon's Hospital was not a medical facility as the epithet "Hospital" was often applied to scholastic establishments that were for boarders only. Although Robert Gordon's College is now arguably the most esteemed school in the Aberdeen area it had very modest beginnings. Robert Gordon was a wealthy Aberdeen merchant who traded with Baltic ports and who left a bequest in his will that money be provided "towards the building of a Hospital and for the maintenance, aliment, entertainment and education of young boys, whose parents are poor and indigent and not be able to maintain them at schools, and put them to trades and employment." While the structure of the main building was completed by 1732 it lay empty for many years until sufficient funds could be raised to complete the interior.

Indeed shortly after this work was finally completed it served a very different purpose as during the second Jacobite uprising the building was commandeered by Hanoverian troops and briefly renamed Fort Cumberland before returning to educational matters. It was during the tutorship of the Rev. Ogilvie that major changes took place. In late 1870's there were new ideas in education and it was felt that poor boys should no longer be segregated in education. So in 1881 application was made for the right to open a fee paying school but to continue to use monies donated by the late Robert Gordon to provide bursaries for the poor. At that same time the facility changed its name to Robert Gordon's College.

Maria was one of eight children, the elder daughter, and came from a very well educated family with her Uncle George becoming headmaster of George Watson's School in Edinburgh, Uncle Joseph lecturing at Aberdeen University while her Uncle William was Rector of Morrison's Academy in Crieff. It was clear from an early age that she was a gifted child and by the time she had reached the age of nine she was sent to the Merchant Company Ladies College in Edinburgh with her sister Emma joining her later.

Maria studied at the school for nine years returning during the summer holidays each year to Aberdeenshire and the family's holiday home in Ballater and spending hours exploring the hills in the company of her brother Francis. In 1888 the Rev. Ogilvie built a large house in that area called Darroch Learg which is now an impressive hotel.

Maria left Merchant College at age eighteen after becoming the school's top scholar and their head girl and being a very gifted pianist she applied to the Royal Academy of Music in London and was accepted. She made such rapid strides that by the end of her first year she had been chosen as the pianist to accompany the Academy's orchestra at public appearances and yet within a year she bored of the course and decided to pursue her first love. Science.

Maria had the good fortune of having friends, or in her case family, in high places as her brother Francis, who was subsequently knighted, was Principal of Heriot-Watt College (now University) in Edinburgh, an establishment not in fact named after its founders but in recognition of Scottish philanthropist and goldsmith George Heriot and Scottish inventor James Watt.

Not surprisingly Maria was accepted and not just because of her sibling as any University would have been delighted to accept the star pupil of the esteemed Merchant Ladies College. She completed the first part of her B.Sc. at Heriot-Watt before heading down south, this time to University College London where in 1890 she received her

D.Sc. degree in geology, botany and zoology, the first woman ever to do so.

Heriot-Watt College in 19th Century Edinburgh

Maria decided to specialise in geology and wanted to begin research work in Germany, applying to the University of Berlin but was turned down as that establishment had a men only policy. Even an intervention by the influential Baron von Richthofen failed to open the door for her. The determined young lady, however, refused to give up and applied to Munich University where two of their top professors agreed to accept her, one of them, Professor Zittel, commenting, somewhat condescendingly, that a Russian female student they had admitted the previous year had listened to his lectures "without causing unacceptable disruption to the University community". Maria studied at that establishment for four years leaving with a Ph.D. and another first as no other female student has previously earned such a degree. The mark she made is recognised to this day with a room in the library of the University being named in her honour.

Baron Ferdinand von Richthofen

The Ogilvie family not only had influential friends in Britain but also in Germany and she was taken under the wing of Baron Ferdinand von Richthofen, who was a Professor of Physical Geography in Berlin and was renowned not only as a scientist but as geographer and traveller. But his family name became known world-wide not through his work and adventures but rather as a result of the exploits of his nephew, Baron Manfred von Richthofen.

Manfred's fame arose from his actions during the First World War, transferring from the German Cavalry to the Air Force in 1915. In no time at all he became widely recognised and respected as an ace pilot and over the course of the next three years the "Red Baron", as he became known, shot down over 80 enemy aircraft. He was quickly established as a national hero in Germany and people would travel to see "Richthofen's Circus" as his unit of fighter aircraft became known because of the way they moved from place to place, living out of hastily erected tents, and as a result of the bright colours of their Fokker planes.

The Red Baron's luck finally ran out on 21 April 1918, only months before the end of the war, when he was shot down over the Somme in France. Since that time he has been the subject of a considerable number of books, more than a dozen movies and has even featured heavily in Charles Shultz *Peanuts* cartoon strip.

Von Richthofen, the scientist not the pilot, encouraged Maria to study the terrain of the Dolomite Mountains in the border region between Austria and Italy and this area of the South Tyrol became her life's work despite its inaccessibility which meant that having university degrees wasn't sufficient and she had to learn how to climb.

The barrenness of the Dolomite Mountains is such that even the chamois (mountain goats) rarely frequent their clefts and tablelands; snow caps them during nine months out of twelve and is perpetual on the highest summits.

Over the course of the next decade she made several trips to this hostile environment and submitted numerous papers on her findings, many written in German further displaying the depth of her education. One was published in the Quarterly Journal of the Geological Society earning her a Doctor of Science from London University. She moved from Munich and enrolled as a private student at the Professor von Zittel Institute allowing her to continue and expand her research and in the process was able to disapprove one of the theories put forward by the revered scientist Charles Darwin.

Her dedication can best be summed up by her work in Austria in the years leading up to 1914 where she spent a considerable period of time on researching and writing a paper. She had just completed the work ready for publication when the First World War broke out and she had to leave the country unable to take anything with her.

She returned to Vienna in 1920 to discover that during the preceding six years the completed paper together with all her notes, maps and surveys had vanished into thin air. Undaunted she set to work and reproduced it although it was seven long years later before it eventually appeared at which time it was described as "A Monument in the Field of Alpine Geology".

Maria and mountain guide Josef Kostner on a field trip

Although she was honoured by memberships from the Vienna Geological Society and Trento University in Italy as well as honorary doctorates from Universities in Innsbruck, Edinburgh and Sydney, she complained about the fact that her work had been largely ignored in England despite producing many papers in the language.

It was a lonely furrow that I ploughed in my field work abroad. A Britisher – and a woman at that – strayed into a remote and mountainous frontier territory between Austria and Italy, a region destined afterwards to be fought over, inch by inch in the Great War.

Despite the fact that she was totally dedicated to her work she did find time in 1895 to marry a Dr. John Gordon and to give birth to four children, John, Coral, Irmgard and Mary although the last named died in infancy. In a case of "if you can't beat them join them" her husband and the three surviving children regularly found themselves trekking after the lady around the mountains of the South Tyrol.

Sadly just short of their silver wedding, John Gordon died in 1919 and despite being an ardent Scot – she made it clear to everyone she met that she was NOT English - Maria moved with her two daughters and her son to London to be near to her brothers Francis, a fellow geologist, and William, a doctor.

That same year the Geological Society of London decided to open its doors to women and Maria was one of the very first females to be admitted. The move to London resulted in her being made a Justice of the Peace and subsequently achieved another distinction when she was made Chairman of the Marylebone Court of Justice, the first woman ever to chair a London Borough Court.

Although geology was her passion Maria had many other interests one of which was politics and she joined the Liberal Party because of its stance on Women's Rights and was chosen as their prospective candidate for the Parliamentary seat of Canterbury but she subsequently withdrew. However, in 1923 she did stand for the Party in Hastings although she came a rather distant second to Unionist candidate Lord Percy. But Maria Gordon's political influence went well beyond these shores as she became engaged in post World War I negotiations at the Council for the Representation of Women in the League of Nations, which subsequently became the United Nations.

That gives a clear indication of the direction that the lady's life took in her later years as she became heavily involved with a number of organisations promoting the rights of women and supporting the burgeoning Suffrage movement. Despite the fact that countries like New Zealand allowed all women over 21 to vote as long ago as 1893, by the start of the 20th century the British political voting system was totally male dominated. For fifty years women's groups had been trying to gain the vote by protesting but were constantly met by politicians with the message that "women are already well represented by their husbands, fathers and sons".

Then on to the scene came Emmiline Pankhurst, a Manchester born political activist who was voted by Time magazine amongst the 100 most influential women of the twenty century. Pankhurst formed the Women's Social and Political Union (WSPU), a group that adopted the simple slogan of "Votes for Women" but decided to pursue this aim in a less than conventional, and many said, less than lady-like manner. The WSPU weren't just content to hand out a few leaflets and make speeches on street corners they went for the "deeds not words" approach in what would now be described as a campaign of civil disobedience.

They chained themselves to railings, tried to storm Parliament and heckled politicians whenever they could, blew up post boxes, smashed shop windows, bombed buildings and regularly ended up in pitched battles with the Police. The establishment and their well behaved tame press ridiculed their actions but what they couldn't ignore was the bravery of the women.

Liberal Party Election Poster

Many were beaten up and even sexually assaulted by the Police and over a thousand of them were arrested and jailed where some continued the struggle by going on hunger strike. The Government's reaction was to force feed the women in the most horrific and inhumane manner, not through any concern for their health but to ensure that the Suffragettes didn't create a martyr that even the establishment's docile press couldn't ignore.

But much as these women suffered, one suffragette paid a far higher price for her beliefs. Emily Davison was born in Greenwich. London in October 1872 and from 1906, when she joined the WSPU, was always at the forefront of the movement. She was arrested nine times, earning a new stripe on the Suffragette label ribbon she wore with pride, went on hunger strike seven times and was force fed forty nine times none of which broke her spirit or reduced her determination to carry on.

On 4 June 1913 Emily travelled by train to the Epsom Race Course in Surrey to attend the Derby, having first collected two flags in the Suffragette colours of purple, green and white from WSPU headquarters. She positioned herself at Tattenham Corner, the final bend before the home straight, and waited until a number of the horses had thundered past before ducking under the rail and walking onto the course carrying her flags.

Emily Davison lying injured on the Epsom race course

She made for the Anmer, King George V's horse, being ridden by a jockey called Herbert Jones, and tried to grab the reins. There are various theories as to what she intended to do, the most plausible being that she was endeavouring to attach a WSPU flag to the horse but what she did succeed in doing was unseating the jockey and bringing the horse down, after it had collided with her while running at great speed. The horse recovered and finished the race without a jockey while Jones and Davison were both rushed to hospital.

Two weeks after the incident Herbert Jones was back racing; two days after the incident Emily Davison was dead as a consequence of a fractured skull. Eleven days later her coffin, shrouded in floral tributes and bearing the message "Fight on. God will give the victory" was paraded through the streets of London followed by a procession of 5000 suffragettes, wearing black armbands in tribute, and several hundred sympathetic men. The route was lined by an estimated 50,000 people and the procession was at last covered by press from around the world.

Emily Davison's funeral

Emily Davison had died for the cause she believed fervently about. In response to the event Queen Mary wrote in her Royal journal that Davison was a "horrid woman" displaying not an ounce of compassion.

Emily Davison's death reported in one of the few sympathetic newspapers

The Suffragette campaign continued undaunted until 1914 when it was suspended because of the outbreak of War, the women dedicating themselves to the war effort and the Government in recognition of this gesture released all suffragettes who had been imprisoned. During the war years the non militant National Union of Woman's Suffrage Society continued to lobby the Government and in February 1918 the Representation of the People Act gave the vote to women over 30 who met "minimum property standards" a giant step forward but still leaving many women disenfranchised.

By 1928, however, that was amended so that all women over 21 were entitled to vote, a right equal to that of the male population.

While Maria was never an active member of WSPU she was a strong supporter of the votes for women movement and became heavily involved with a number of different organisations. She was Vice President of the International Council of Women, and Honorary President of both the Associated Women's Friendly Society and the National Women's Citizens Association. However it was with the National Council of Women of Great Britain and Northern Ireland that she became most associated, being voted their President in 1916.

With her advancing years she was no longer able to carry out arduous field trips but her work was not forgotten. In 1931 she remarkably achieved yet another first when the Geological Society of Austria granted her the honour of being their first ever honorary female member and a year later her considerable achievements in the field was recognised by the Geological Society of London when she was awarded the Lyell Medal. An even greater honour lay ahead, however, when in 1935 she was awarded the D.B.E. and became Dame Maria Ogilvie-Gordon.

Dame Maria Ogilvie-Gordon's gravestone at Allenvale Cemetery

On 24th June 1939 while living a relatively quiet life in the Regent's Park area of London she died. Her funeral service was held in London where she was cremated but at her request her ashes were returned to her native North East of Scotland and were interned in a grave in Allenvale Cemetery in Aberdeen alongside that of her husband and Mary, her infant child.

But that is not quite the end of the story. As recently as 17 May 2018 a new 3D visualisation centre was opened at Heriot-Watt University, a joint venture between the University, the Oil and Gas Authority and the British Geological Society. The world class facility is known as the Ogilvie-Gordon 3D Visualisation Centre, a fitting and lasting tribute to the "firsts" lady.

Lorna Moon
(1886-1930)

Scatter My Ashes on Mormond Hill

On a sunny but breezy Aberdeenshire day in the summer of 1930 two figures walked slowly and reverently down Mormond Hill past the famous white horse etched onto the hillside. The younger man gazed with a mixture of awe and bemusement at the sleepy village below. The older man, stooping slightly because of his advancing years, cradled a small polished wooden box in his arms. Not a word passed between the men until they reached the outskirts of the village.

"Thanks for comin' a' this wiy son. Here's yer box" said the older man.

"Why don't you keep it sir" was the response.

"Are you sure you dinna wint to tak' it hame wi' you? It's a grand box."

"Quite sure sir"

"Well be assured young loon that I will pit it to good use. I think it wid be richt handy to keep my shoe cleaning stuff in."

The elderly man was Charles Low; the younger Everett Marcy.

Charlie Low was born illegitimate, his mother Mary Ann Low being a maid in an Aberdeenshire mansion. On the birth certificate the father is listed as Charles May, a fellow servant, although speculation suggests that a member of the aristocracy might have been involved, happy to step aside while everyone assumed that "the Butler did it". What is certainly known is that Mary Ann subsequently married a Police detective called Samuel Flint and they moved to London where they set up home but, in what was perhaps an early example of a Low family trait, they didn't take young Charles with them.

Instead Charles was despatched to his grandparents who lived in the Aberdeenshire village of Broadsea on the outskirts of Fraserburgh and that was where he grew up. After leaving the local school Charles trained as a house plasterer and subsequently moved to Strichen where he met and married a mill worker called Margaret Benzies.

The couple ran the Temperance Hotel in Strichen, an establishment frequented by commercial travellers traversing the hinterland of North East Scotland with their assorted wares. In truth Margaret was often left to run the hotel on her own as her husband travelled as far afield as America, Canada and even South Africa in search of plastering work. He was, however, better known for his political views, a staunch socialist who was in regular correspondence with MPs at Westminster and who held meetings with those of a similar left wing persuasion in a shed at the rear of the Temperance Hotel.

These get-togethers became so well known that a local wag referred to the shed as "10 Downing Street" and the name stuck, so much so that in the late 19th century if you sent a letter addressed to 'Charles Low Esq., 10 Downing Street, Strichen, Aberdeenshire' the postman would deliver it to the shed. He was an atheist which was an unusual and no doubt unpopular stance in a village with a population of about 800 where all three churches were packed on a Sunday morning.

A bust of Charles Low on display in Strichen Library

The couple had five children with their second daughter being born on 16 June 1886 and named Helen Nora Wilson Low. Nora, as the young girl became know, attended the local Episcopal School receiving what she later described as "a very ordinary education" and seemingly enjoying the school holidays far more. She would regularly spend these in Broadsea staying with a relative, George Low Cameron, and her love of the seaside meant that she was always very reluctant to return to Strichen when the holidays were over.

Nora left the school for the last time in 1900 when she turned fourteen and began work at that tender age, assisting her Mother in running the Hotel. It was in that very establishment that several years later Nora met a gentleman by the name of William Hebditch.

Hebditch was a watchmaker who hailed from Selby in Yorkshire and who was a regular guest at the Temperance Hotel. Despite a substantial age difference – in 1907 Nora was 21 and Hebditch 29 - they became more than good friends and on the 24 December of that year the couple secretly stole away and were married in the Registry Office in Aberdeen.

They set up their marital home in Yorkshire where Nora gave birth to a son named William after his Father although always referred to as Bill. During that period in the early Twentieth Century the Canadian Government were providing incentives to anyone willing to emigrate to their sparsely populated country and the Hebditch family took up this offer and sailed across the Atlantic to a new life.

They settled in Entwhistle in Alberta, a proper frontier or hick town which had only just been established as a settlement. Even today Entwhistle is hardly a metropolis with a population of less than four hundred. It is difficult to know exactly what Nora expected to find in this new world; after all she hadn't exactly been brought up in the lap of luxury in Scotland. Nevertheless Entwhistle proved to be quite a shock as the cabin they inhabited was beyond basic without even running water and Nora regularly had to collect pails of water from a nearby burn while the hamlet at that time appeared to boast more bears than people.

There was just the one local store in Entwhistle run by a gentleman called Walter Moon. Moon was also an immigrant from Yorkshire and a friendship ensued between him and the Hebditch family. Unfortunately, for William anyway, the relationship between Walter Moon and Nora Low went beyond conventional friendship and Nora, who hadn't travelled half way round the world for this life of boredom and hardship, secretly plotted with the store keeper for them to leave Entwhistle together.

For many women there would have been a major obstacle in the form of a son, now five years old, but it was clear from this and future actions, that Nora didn't possess strong maternal instincts. She simply waited until William was away on business and wrote a letter to him explaining her actions, that she wouldn't be returning and that she had left Bill for him to bring up as "he always liked you more than me anyway". She then left the note, and the little boy, with a neighbour and departed Entwhistle with Walter Moon.

She never saw her son again.

The couple had decided to travel right to the centre of Canada, to Winnipeg a town that was known as the gateway to the West. With a population of close on a hundred thousand at that time Winnipeg was not only a total contrast to Entwhistle but at last provided Nora with the bright lights she craved to see.

Being already married it was clear that they couldn't legally wed but as it was unheard of at that time for an unmarried couple to live or even travel together, she took Moon's name. Despite having a fairly basic education Nora had always been an avid reader and one of her great literary heroines was Lorna Doone, a character created by author R.D. Doddridge, and so she thought, if she was going to change her surname why not go the whole hog? And so, aged twenty seven, Lorna Moon was born.

In Winnipeg Lorna found work as a journalist contributing articles on a variety of subjects for a local paper although specialising in film reviews. She also gave birth to a baby girl they called Mary Leonora Moon; clearly, however, Walter was as unimpressed by parenthood as his partner and aged six months Mary was despatched with a nurse back to England to be raised by Moon's family.

Lorna never saw the girl again although in later life Mary Moon endeavoured to follow in her mother's footsteps, travelling to Hollywood and seeking work as screenwriter albeit with considerably less success. She also wrote a book titled *Ogopogo: The Okanagan Mystery* about a Canadian version of the Loch Ness monster which according to Indian legend lives in Lake Okanagan in British Columbia. Unburdened by children Walter and Lorna moved to Minneapolis where Lorna continued her career as a journalist, and in what was the golden era of Hollywood Lorna, like so many other people in America, became an ardent cinema goer.

Cecil B. DeMille

The greatest movie mogul of the time was Cecil B. DeMille who over the course of an illustrious career was involved as producer or director of over seventy films, both in the silent and talkies eras, becoming the most commercially successful person in the history of cinema. He was also the co-founder of Paramount Pictures. DeMille was born in Ashfield, Massachusetts and was originally a stage actor before trying his hand at directing. His directorial debut *The Squaw Man,* released in 1914, was the first feature length film made in Hollywood.

In 1919 DeMille produced a film titled *Male and Female* starring one of the great stars of the day, Gloria Swanson. During the 1920's Swanson, who is remembered to this day as the original Norma Desmond in Billy Wilder's wonderful *Sunset Boulevard,* was earning a remarkable $20,000 a week and is believed to have earned eight million dollars during her career. Unfortunately for her, she managed to spend eight million dollars on a hugely extravagant life style.

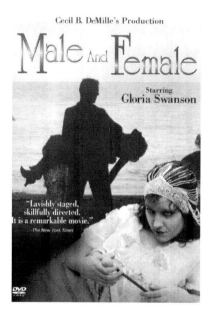

As a consequence of Swanson's involvement *Male and Female* was a huge box office draw, netting more than a million dollars but despite that Lorna was far from impressed by the movie. Now most cinema goers of that era would simply have gone home disappointed – after all there was no IMDB where you could vent your ire in those days. But whatever else Lorna was she was never one of the crowd and so she got out her pad and wrote to Cecil B. DeMille, telling him in no uncertain terms how unimpressed she was with his latest work or "razzed him wickedly" as she later described her actions.

What caused Lorna to take such action has never been fully explained but it could certainly be connected to the fact that *Male and Female* was an adaption of the book *The Admirable Crichton* written by one of Lorna's great literary heroes, J. M. Barrie. Perhaps it was simply her dissatisfaction with the Hollywood treatment of one of her favourite books that prompted her to write but whatever the reason she was more than a little taken aback by what transpired.

For much to her surprise, Mister DeMille replied and, no doubt with his tongue firmly placed in his cheek, suggested that if she thought she could do better why didn't she come to Hollywood and give it a try? Not the wisest thing to say to someone like Lorna who once again got out her trusty writing materials, scribbled a "Dear Walter" letter and headed for Hollywood.

The Hollywood that Lorna arrived in was very different from the 21st Century version we all know with its glitzy awards ceremonies adorned by red carpets, ten thousand dollar dresses and vacuous, teary acceptance speeches thanking half of the population of California. Go back yet another thirty years to the late 19th Century, however, and the area was nothing more than barren wasteland, ten miles from the vibrant city of Los Angeles. Then a property developer by the name of H. J. Whitley bought 480 acres of scrub land and set about establishing a new town.

The name Hollywood derived from nearby Holly Canyon. The community grew slowly until in 1903 it was incorporated as a municipality and two months later the citizens of Hollywood, obviously keen to ensure that their little town didn't copy the worst excesses of their much larger neighbour, banned the sale of alcohol in Hollywood. You will not be surprised to learn that the by-law was subsequently revoked. By 1910 Hollywood had become part of the expanding municipality of Los Angeles and the name of the small town's main thoroughfare was changed from Prospect Avenue to the somewhat more glamorous Hollywood Boulevard.

In the early part of the 20th Century the blossoming movie industry was largely centred in New Jersey but the prospect of better weather for filming and spectacular backdrops right on their doorsteps attracted film makers who decided to "go west young man" and studios began to pop up in and around the still sparsely populated Hollywood area. The 1920's were the boom era for Hollywood as America was about to enter 'The Roaring Twenties', a decade when the average American was enjoying the benefits of the country's prosperity, abruptly brought to a sudden halt by the Wall Street Crash in 1929, and enjoyed spending part of their new found wealth in going to the movies.

It was that prosperous climate that greeted Lorna when she arrived on the West Coast just prior to the erection of the famous sign built on a hill overlooking the town. Originally the sign read "Hollywoodland" and was designed to publicise a new housing development and not the movie industry.

She quickly secured a position with DeMille's Famous Players Lasky-Paramount Picture Company (subsequently sensibly abridged to Paramount Pictures) as a script girl. DeMille must have spotted real talent in Lorna as before long she was working as a script writer on a new movie titled *The Affairs of Anatol.*

Lorna instantly immersed herself in the glamorous scene, rubbing shoulders with the great and the good, and also the not so good, of Hollywood at swanky parties and soirees. One of the men she met at such an event was William deMille. William deMille (despite the slightly different spelling of the surname) was Cecil B. DeMille's older brother. He was a very successful playwright, with a string of stage works to his name as well as a screenwriter and film director. He was also married to Anna with whom he had two children.

William deMille

In 1921 Hollywood was reeling from the Fatty Arbuckle scandal and rumours of other unsavoury events and Cecil B. DeMille was concerned by the effect on his own persona if it became public knowledge that his married brother was having an affair with a married, albeit estranged, screenwriter contracted to Paramount. If that gave him sleepless nights he must have been apoplectic when William revealed to him that Lorna was pregnant and that he was the father.

During an examination whilst she was pregnant with deMille's child it was discovered that Lorna was suffering from tuberculosis, thought to have been originally contacted due to the damp conditions in her native Strichen. The doctor concluded that she was not strong enough to give birth and proposed an immediate termination. Lorna, in an uncharacteristic outburst of maternal instinct, totally refused to have an abortion and declared that she was going to have the baby and that the child "would have the deMille name".

On 12 February 1922 in Monrovia, California Lorna gave birth to a boy who was named Richard. For health reasons the boy was taken from his mother immediately after he was born and subsequently placed in an orphanage. Lorna Moon never saw her son again. Six months later Cecil and Constance DeMille attended the orphanage and adopted Richard as their son. The boy got the famous name; Lorna got her wish.

For reasons best known to them, the family decided that Richard would not be told that the man he called Uncle Willie was in fact his biological father and it was only in 1955 when William deMille died that Richard, by then aged 33, was informed of the truth about both his father and his mother. Clearly fascinated by her remarkable life, Richard set to work writing a book about Lorna which was published in 1998 under the title *My Secret Mother: Lorna Moon*. He also wrote a brief introduction to the 2002 volume *The Collected Works of Lorna Moon* and, shortly before he died in 2009, made a pilgrimage to the North East of Scotland to see where his mother was born and where her ashes had been scattered.

Richard deMille

Despite her ill health Lorna continued to work and to make a name for herself among the Hollywood elite and during the early part of the 1920's her name appeared in the credits to a host of films such as *Don't Tell Everything, Her Husband's Trademark* and *Too Much Wife*. It was in the years 1926 and 1927, however, that she achieved the distinction of becoming one of the highest paid, if not THE highest paid, female screenwriter in Hollywood and this coincided with her association with some of the biggest names in the movie business such as Lon Chaney.

Chaney earned the epithet "The Man of A Thousand Faces" due to his ability to don make up and transform himself into a variety of strange and often grotesque characters such as the *Hunchback of Notre Dame* and the *Phantom of the Opera*. One of his biggest successes came with *Mr. Wu*, a movie about a Chinese patriarch who vows revenge on an Englishman who seduced his daughter. Lorna produced the screen play, adapting a stage play of the same name.

But the success at the box office of *Mr. Wu* was eclipsed later in 1927 when Lorna adapted Tolstoy's book *Anna Karenina* for the screen in the movie *Love*. Surely only Hollywood could take a title as enigmatic as *Anna Karenina* and come up with something so mundane as *Love*. They obviously realised the error of their ways in 1935 when this silent movie was remade as a talkie, this time opting for the title of *Anna Karenina*.

Both versions starred Greta Garbo, the Swedish-American actress who remains one of the most famous Hollywood stars of all time albeit often remembered for her celebrated quote "I want to be alone" as much as the host of films she starred in. In later life Garbo pointed out that what she had actually said "I want to be LET alone... there is all the difference". In many ways she got her wish as she never married although she was living with frequent co-star John Gilbert when she made *Love*.

The draw of the name Garbo proved irresistible to audiences and the movie grossed close on a million dollars in the U.S. alone and nearly twice that worldwide, further enhancing the Lorna Moon reputation. Sadly her ill health meant that *Love* was the zenith of Lorna's Hollywood career.

Back before her meteoric rise to fame with Paramount, Lorna had already tried her hand at writing, and for once not in the form of a farewell letter to a husband but with a simple short story. *Silk Both Sides* was the first ever introduction to Drumorty, a fictional village created by Lorna, a thinly disguised Strichen.

Silk Both Sides is a charming if ultimately poignant tale of two people living out their lonely lives, a cottar man called Jock Sclessor and a spinster called Jessie MacLean. Every Sunday they walk to and from Church together and every Sunday Jessie, and the whole of Drumorty for that matter, wait for Jock to propose. But the problem is that Jock is a scutterer who realises that if he is going to take a wife that he is going to have to extend his little cottar house and that places him in the horns of a dilemma as he had to decide "whether to level the rowan tree and build it on the east – or move the peats and build it on the west".

This situation goes on for many years until Jessie decides that enough is enough and goes to the local drapery and buys two and a half yards of four inch satin ribbon, "silk both sides". The significance of this choice is beautifully examined by Lorna; "a satin faced ribbon might have many uses but silk both sides was a bonnet string by all the laws of millinery known to Drumorty". And the only person who would ever wear a bonnet tied beneath the chin with silk ribbon was a confirmed spinster. This marvellous piece of writing tells a heartfelt story in a mere four brief pages in a manner which many books would fail to achieve in an hundred.

Lorna sent the short story to the New York Century magazine which published it in 1920 and despite the fact that the story was partly written in Scots and Doric, it was well received in America. Buoyed by this success she began to pen more stories of Drumorty life.

Over the course of the next few years Lorna wrote a further seven stories varying in subject from the humorous to the achingly sad but with one thing in common; wonderfully drawn characters and brilliantly observed vignettes of life in a claustrophobic small village where gossip was the chief currency.

The humour comes from the likes of *The Corp*, a superb insight into the pettiness of small village life. Kirsty Fraser has been the main "crier" at funerals in Drumorty for forty five years, her abilities as a keener developing with each and every burial until she was able to have fits right over the coffin. But disaster struck when Sandy McNab died suddenly and his widow refused to have Kirsty at the funeral due to the fact that she had openly scoffed at Mistress McNab's butter at Drumorty show and flaunted the fact that hers had won first prize. And so, in the blink of an eye Kirsty's elevated position as Drumorty's chief mourner disappeared. There is a very different tone to *The Funeral*, the basic premise of which was undoubtedly inspired by Lorna's own father as the character of Tammas MacBride is the local plasterer who heads off to America to look for work although in the fictional tale he leaves behind a wife tending for a very ill young son. The story is a brilliant demonstration of how pride and concern for what the neighbours think can have disastrous results.

The remaining stories vary in both style and content from the naive *The Courtin' of Sally Ann,* where Lorna somewhat strangely doesn't give the lad doing the courtin' a name but simply calls him "the gype", to the dark and almost grisly *Wantin' A Hand* where the main character is, just as the title suggests, short of an appendage.

But one story stands head and shoulders above all the rest. *The Sinning of Jessie MacLean* reunites the reader with the spinster lady with the bonnet tied beneath her chin and shows her to be an island of goodness and compassion amidst a sea of tittle-tattle and hypocrisy.

Jessie is leading a quiet and uneventful life until the good and Godly people of Drumorty turn their wrath on Bella Tocher, a slip of a girl who works at Skilly's farm. Bella's crime that arouses such fury in the multitude is falling pregnant while unmarried. The citizens are not just content to drum Bella out of the village but insist on making an example of her by forcing her to walk down the main street to the railway station with the window blinds on every window she passes being pulled down forcibly to display how everyone is shunning her.

Like sheep the house occupants follow these instructions with the sole exception of Miss MacLean who not only rescues the girl from the ordeal but gives her shelter under her roof. The reserved and placid Jessie suddenly finds a cause worth fighting for and her voice as is displayed in a wonderful speech provided to her by the writer when Jessie is confronted by Skilly who is willing to take Bella back, at half the wages of course, if the girl is repentant and "makes admission of her sins".

Her sins? It's no her sins that Drumorty is punishin' her for. It's the evidence, Skilly. It's the bairn. There's them that sit on the elder's bench and gie judgement that ken more o' sin than Bella Tocher but they dinna get found oot; the siller in the collection plate blinds the minister.

The Sinning of Jessie MacLean show the vividness of the writing and makes you wonder just what she could have achieved as an author if her life hadn't been so tragically cut short.

These seven stories were again picked up by the Century magazine and reprinted elsewhere and the manner in which they were received by readers of these publications gave rise to the demand for a book. Having engaged a literary agent who in turn attracted a publisher, the stories were neatly packaged in a book which saw the light of day under the title of *Doorways in Drumorty*.

As mentioned before, Lorna was a great admirer of the writer J.M. Barrie. Barrie, best known for the ageless *Peter Pan,* was born in Kirriemuir in Angus and wrote a number of books set in his native town which he renamed Thrums, a name that remains to this day. Wander around Kirremuir and you will come across the Thrums Hotel, the Thrums Take Away and even the Thrums Veterinary Clinic.

Probably the best known of these books is *A Window in Thrums* and it has long been assumed that Lorna came up with the title *Doorways in Drumorty* as a sort of tribute. However in a letter written by her to Hewitt Hanson Howland, her agent, from the Plaza Hotel in fashionable Union Square, San Francisco on 25 May 1925 Lorna comments "I like the title *Doorways in Drumorty* very much, it looks and sounds well", suggesting it was the rather grandly named Mr Howland who came up with it rather than Lorna.

Irrespective of its origins that was the title used for Lorna's first full literary work and *Doorways in Drumorty* was published in Indianapolis in 1925 and in London the following year. It enjoyed rave reviews and healthy sales and was universally well received. Well almost universally. Jist nae in Strichen.

In creating the host of characters that inhabit Drumorty, Lorna had clearly drawn on people she had known during her time in Strichen and despite the fact that she had changed the names, folk recognised themselves and on the whole weren't best pleased by the manner in which they were depicted. It is rumoured that even her father was less than impressed by his daughter's description of Strichen life despite the fact that the book was dedicated "To my Dad, this his wee Nottie's first book".

In the stage play *Doorways in Drumorty* which was adapted from the book, Mistress MacKenty has a lengthy conversation with a new Librarian who, much to the chagrin of the locals has decided not only to stock the book in the library but also to promote it. This brief snippet from the script perhaps best sums up the villagers' reaction:

Are you suggesting that this Nora Low is telling lies about the local people?

Now hing on. I niver suggested that fit she's written is untrue. Jist insulting

Whatever the reason, the locals felt sufficiently strongly that they persuaded the local library to ban the book. Not just for a week or two but for years, over fifty years in fact with it only appearing on the shelves of the Strichen Library in the 1980's when a new edition was brought out by David Toulmin. Today the village of Strichen is proud of their most famous daughter and there are small blue plaques on two of the buildings as a memorial to her. But peer behind the modern day version of the chintz curtains and you will still encounter people who will tell you that the "hiv nae time for thon Nora Low quine."

As her success both as a screenwriter and author increased her health deteriorated and she spent the first six months of 1928 in the Hillcrest Sanatorium in Tujanga, La Crescenta, California, a far cry from the Christie Hotel in Hollywood and the fancy apartments in San Francisco and Los Angeles that she was used to residing in. Early in 1929 Lorna travelled to a sanatorium in Albuquerque, New Mexico in the hope that the dry warm climate might be beneficial for her health and sadly this became her home for the rest of her all too short life.

It was in this medical facility that Lorna decided to write a novel, one that would be published later that year under the title *Dark Star.* It is a very different piece of work to *Doorways,* dark by name and dark by nature, as is clear from the first sentence – "Nancy was glad when her grandmother died". Hardly a conventional opening but then again little about Lorna was conventional.

The main storyline was undoubtedly inspired by the circumstances of her own father's birth as the principal character of Nancy is revealed as being born illegitimately to a maid in a mansion house who won't disclose whether the girl's father was a fellow servant, the groom, or a member of the wealthy family who own the house and Nancy is anxious to discover the truth, desperately hoping that the blood of aristocracy flows through her veins. This gives rise to the novel's title as is explained:

But woe betide the bairn that is born under a dark star, for she is forever taking the wrong turn in the road. Her simplest move takes on an evil look and is held against her for a sin....and love never shows its face but it comes sharp-thorned with grief.

Rather too much of the book is given over to lengthy, and at times rather tedious "he loves me, he loves me not" exchanges between Nancy and a character initially just called the "Whistling Boy", turning it almost into a sort of Mills & Buchan.

There are times, however, when it comes to life as with the arrival of Divot Meg, so called as she makes her living touring around the countryside with a cart pulled by a donkey selling divots, or large pieces of turf, to anyone wanting to protect their winter stock of potatoes from the frost and snow. She introduces the reader to an amazing set of worthies, characters that Dickens at his most imaginative would have been proud of.

Meg runs a very "doon market" boarding house frequented by a motley selection of wandering waifs and strays and it is here that the fun begins. We are introduced to Tinker Tam with his bundle, carried on a stick over his shoulder, which is opened out to display an interesting assortment of food items, pretty much all stolen and the Cauld Rice Piper man, who has an oilskin bag full of all kinds of rice, including rice pudding, which he consumes, not surprisingly bearing in mind his nick name, cold.

Entertainment is provided for the assembled crowd by the likes of Rose-Eyes, so called because of his love of singing a song of that name, who performs within a circle of paraffin oil, created to ensure that the body lice that he boasts in abundance don't leave him and find another body to occupy. It is clear from Lorna's brief description of Divot Meg's home that it is hardly salubrious with the guests gathering in an evening in the "tinker's kitchen". The house does, however, boast a front bedroom with a wooden bedstead and any man who rented that was not only entitled to use of the frying pan first but also "other privileges of a more intimate nature", one of several racy comments, well certainly racy by 1920's standards, that permeate the book.

There is also a wonderful *Drumorty* type story of Janet Clark, who runs a boarding house for "selected gentleman", one of whom is Mister Robertson the local bank manager. He comments on how the lace of her dress beautifully frames her hand and Miss Clark spends the next fifteen years adorning all her clothes in the same manner hoping, in vain, for him to repeat the compliment. There is, however, a happy ending including an extremely mannered proposal scene that displays Lorna's writing style at its best.

Dark Star comes to a dramatic, and quite shocking, conclusion and taken on its own terms it is an enjoyable read; it is only when compared with the joys of *Drumorty* that it appears uneven and lacking the heights of humour and depths of despair that make Lorna's first book such a joy not just to read but to return to again and again.

Writing the book proved an arduous process for Lorna due to her failing health and in truth it would probably never have seen the light of day had it not been for her friend, Frances Marion. Indeed the book was dedicated by Lorna to her friend adding in "Note – all the characters in this novel are imaginary" perhaps a comment aimed at the people of Strichen.

Frances Marion was a fellow screenwriter who went on to enjoy great success with all aspects of film making including directing. She wrote a remarkable 325 scripts, was the first writer of either sex to win two Academy Awards and wrote extensively during her early career for Mary Pickford, the darling of the silent screen. In fact she became such good friends with Mary that the two girls honeymooned together when Francis married actor Fred Thomson, her third husband, and Mary wed Douglas Fairbanks.

Mary Pickford and Frances Marion

Frances Marion Thomson, as she was then known, was also a very good friend to Lorna Moon and indeed Lorna stayed with her in her home in Beverley Hills in December 1928 before heading off to the sanatorium. While many other acquaintances in Hollywood would no doubt have forgotten about Lorna after she was ensconced in the wilds of New Mexico, Frances visited her regularly.

As a consequence of her illness there were days when Lorna was unable to write and Frances paid secretaries to attend the sanatorium and take down and transcribe the book being dictated to them by Lorna. But her involvement with *Dark Star* may have gone even further as there are suggestions that Frances might have written sections of the book when her friend was laid so low that she wasn't even able dictate.

The book was finished and published in 1929 and despite its dark and sombre themes enjoyed excellent reviews and achieved healthy sales. It was at this stage that Frances, in an effort to raise money to meet Lorna's crippling medical expenses, floated the idea to MGM of a movie based on *Dark Star.*

MGM were on the lookout for a vehicle to help resurrect the flagging career of one of their biggest names, Wallace Beery. Frances Marion, who agreed to co-write the screenplay, was successful in persuading MGM to commission the picture although they were insistent that the whole mood be changed and that she produce a comedy. Only Hollywood could transform a moody and atmospheric work titled *Dark Star* into a comedy called *Min and Bill.*

The resultant film can at best be described as "loosely based" on Lorna's book although some of the characters like Nancy and Bella Pringle retain their original names. Set in a fishing port, Beery plays the Bill of the title with Marie Dresser as Min. Dresser was another actor down on her luck, the parts she enjoyed during the silent era having dried up, but aged 59 she returned to the silver screen triumphantly, picking up an Academy Award for her portrayal of Min.

The movie was a great success, netting a profit of a remarkable £731,000, a great deal of money in 1930. It also proved a watershed for Beery who, on the strength of the success of the movie, managed to have a clause added to his contract to the effect that he would be paid $1 more than any other actor under contract to the studio.

MGM were so delighted with *Min and Bill* that they immediately sought a sequel reuniting Beery and Dresser in *Tugboat Annie* which even surpassed its predecessor financially bringing home a profit of more than million dollars although neither Lorna Moon nor Frances Marion were involved with it. While audiences loved *Min and Bill* we can only speculate what Lorna would have made of this unusual adaption of her novel as on 1 May 1930 Lorna suffered a haemorrhage in the Sanatorium and died. She was forty four years of age and the third book which, days earlier she had been telling visitors she intended writing, was not to be.

At the time of her death she was regularly visited by a young American man called Everett Marcy, an admirer of her work and, in all likelihood, a boyfriend. Aware that her time was short, she asked Everett if he would arrange for her to be cremated in Albuquerque and that he take her ashes back to Scotland and scatter them on

Mormond Hill. It was a great deal to ask of someone so young to travel from the South West of the U.S.A. to the North East of Scotland but he agreed, displaying the power and charisma of Lorna Moon from beyond the grave.

The box used to carry Lorna Moon's ashes

Lorna was cremated as requested and her ashes interned in a small oak box and carried reverently by the young man to Strichen before being scattered by Marcy and Charles Low on Mormond Hill.

In 2002 Black and White books published a volume entitled *The Collected Works of Lorna Moon*. It contained *Doorways in Drumorty* and *Dark Star* as well as an interesting short biography by Glenda Norquay, a number of letters Lorna had written and several poems. It is fitting to allow Lorna the final word with an unpublished and untitled poem, which appears to have been written during her final days while bed ridden in the Sanatorium.

If ever I rise up again and walk the busy street,
If ever I rise up again with eager lightsome feet,
If ever I can breast the wind or bide the lashing rain,
Or feel the sea upon my face, and meet my friends again,
Oh if that day will ever come when I can walk on grass,
And smell the mouldy smell of earth and watch a bird fly past,
I'll be a better girl – maybe. But maybe I'll be worse,
It isn't in me to be good, except inside a hearse.

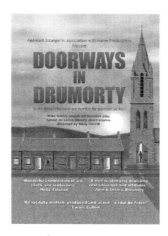

The Red Rag Theatre Company premiered a stage play adapted from Lorna's book at the Lemon Tree Theatre in Aberdeen in 2010 before undertaking a short tour of rural North East venues and a sold out performance at the Dundee Rep Theatre. Buoyed by its success Red Rag undertook a major Scottish tour the following year with two of the original cast, Fraser Sivewright and Michelle Bruce and with Belle Jones replacing Anne Kane Howie. It again enjoyed wonderful audience feedback and press reviews at the likes of Perth Theatre, the Byre St Andrews and the Eden Court Inverness as well as a string of smaller spaces.

Original 2010 cast

2019 tour cast

In spring 2019 the Edinburgh based theatre company Awkward Stranger staged a new production travelling to 18 different venues the length and breadth of Scotland. The show was directed by Andy Corelli and starred Fraser Sivewright, Estrid Barton and Lucy Goldie.

To coincide with the 2019 tour Mike Gibb wrote and published a new book titled *Drumorty Revisited* in which Lorna's characters come back to life in an expanded version of *The Sinning of Jessie MacLean* and eight new stories of Drumorty life. Proceeds from the book, which sells for £5.99, go to help the Bianca dog and cat rescue shelter. For further information on the play or the book contact the writer at mikegibb32@outlook.com or on 07903 463163.

The Doric Board (North-East Tradition and Language) was formed in 2019 as the successor to the North-East Scots Language Board, which had been set up at the instigation of Aberdeen University's Elphinstone Institute and the Robert Gordon University.

The main aim of The Doric Board is to promote the wonderful and unique heritage of language, music, ballad, song, story, history and lore indigenous to the North-east corner of Scotland.

The Board members are volunteers, many of whom have spent a lifetime studying and promoting the culture of the North-east and they bring a wealth of diverse talent to the Board. The stated objective of the Board is: "through advocacy, campaigning, education, public programming, funding and sustained research, to enhance linguistic and cultural confidence in the North-East, being a powerful voice for social, and economic, regeneration, and a driver towards a national Scots Language Board. The Board aims to create and support a sustainable, dynamic future for North-East Scots as a vibrant language, increasingly respected across the region in the context of a diverse and open society."

In its first year, the Board awarded a number of grants to individuals, groups and organisations throughout the area to assist the funding of projects which foster the language and culture of the North-east, one of which is the publication of this work.

The Doric Board is delighted to be associated with "Forgotten Heroines of the North-East", from the pen of Mike Gibb, one of the area's most respected writers.

For further information on the work of the Doric Board go to info@doricboard.com.

Gordon M Hay

Member of The Doric Board

Associação de Protecção aos Animais sem Lar do Concelho de Sesimbra
IBAN PT50003507710001636053029   BIC CGDIPTPL

All proceeds from the sale of this book will be donated to the Bianca Charity which has operated a rescue shelter in Sesimbra, Portugal for over fifteen years and year after year cares for and rehomes hundreds of stray and abandoned dogs and cats. At the time of writing they have over 400 dogs and 100 cats in their care,

For further information about the shelter and its work go to https://www.bianca.pt/english/

The shelter also runs a Holiday & Help scheme for anyone interested in enjoying a holiday in beautiful Sesimbra, a fishing village and beach resort just south of Lisbon, combining it with helping out at the shelter. For further information contact Mike Gibb at biancaambassador@gmail.com.